Co-op, Condo, or Townhouse

Everything
You Need to Know
Before Buying a
Co-op, Condo, or
Townhouse

KEN ROTH

American Management Association

New York • Atlanta • Brussels • Chicago • Mexico City • San Francisco
Shanghai • Tokyo • Toronto • Washington, D.C.

Special discounts on bulk quantities of AMACOM books are available to corporations, professional associations, and other organizations. For details, contact Special Sales Department, AMACOM, a division of American Management Association, 1601 Broadway, New York, NY 10019.
Tel.: 212-903-8316. Fax: 212-903-8083.
Website: www. amacombooks.org

This publication is designed to provide accurate and authoritative information in regard to the subject matter covered. It is sold with the understanding that the publisher is not engaged in rendering legal, accounting, or other professional service. If legal advice or other expert assistance is required, the services of a competent professional person should be sought.

The stories and examples used in this book are general compilations of events and stories that we have heard about or experienced in more than 25 years in the real estate profession. They are structured to illustrate specific teaching points. Any resemblance to actual events or persons is coincidental. In other words, if you think we are talking about you, we aren't.

Various names used by companies to distinguish their software and other products can be claimed as trademarks. AMACOM uses such names throughout this book for editorial purposes only, with no intention of trademark violation. All such software or product names are in initial capital letters or ALL CAPITAL letters. Individual companies should be contacted for complete information regarding trademarks and registration.

REALTOR® is a registered collective membership mark that identifies a real estate professional who is a member of the NATIONAL ASSOCIATION of REALTORS® and subscribes to its strict code of ethics.

Library of Congress Cataloging-in-Publication Data

Roth, Kenneth M.
     Everything you need to know before buying a co-op, condo, or townhouse / Ken Roth.
       p.   cm.
   Includes index.
   ISBN-10: 0-8144-7325-3
   ISBN-13: 978-0-8144-7325-2
   1. Real estate investment.   2. House buying.   I. Title.

   HD1382.5.R68   2006
   643'.12—dc22   2006008605

Printing number

10   9   8   7   6   5   4   3   2

Also, honorable mention to my grandchildren,
Erika (12), Paula (10), Martin (10), and Danny (8).
They are outstanding, and we are very proud of them.

Before Buying a Co-op, Condo, or Townhouse

INTRODUCTION

My first recollections of residential living were as a child. My parents and I lived in a two-bedroom, two-bath apartment in the town of Rego Park in the borough of Queens, New York City.

I knew, perhaps instinctively, that we lived in a nice building, nicer than others on the block. Our building appeared newer; it had a uniformed doorman and a superintendent, complete with leather tool belt worn loosely, "gunslinger style" on his hip, and pack of cigarettes folded in his tee-shirt sleeve. The superintendent had an assistant who rarely spoke and whose main function appeared to be mopping the lobby floors.

I knew we paid rent, and realized that we didn't own the apartment because my parents would often discuss buying a house. This meant week-end excursions to such Meccas of New York City suburban living as Cedar-hurst and Great Neck, which were just outside the city limits, where you could visit such edifices as *split-levels, ranches,* and *colonial-style houses.* My father dismissed the other type of home ownership, which consisted of a row of private homes connected or attached by a common wall and inex-plicably referred to as *semi-detached housing.* My father said that this type of housing was neither an apartment nor a private house, and it made no sense to purchase one.

There was one building in the neighborhood that my mother always referred to in whispers, as if it were some sort of house of ill repute. This was the *co-op*. I remember walking with her and her friends. When we passed that building, she would say in hushed tones, as if wanting to protect my tender ears from blasphemy, that so-and-so lives there, but "it's a co-op."

TIMES HAVE CHANGED

Today, our faithful doorman is referred to as a *concierge*. The superintendent has been replaced by a *building engineer*. The taciturn assistant who mopped the floors is now a member of the building maintenance staff, and semi-detached homes are now *townhouses*.

Residential home ownership is no longer limited to ranches, split-levels, and colonials, but rather, there is a dizzying array of choices for the real estate investor. You can choose between not only houses, but also condominiums, the heretofore-mysterious co-ops or cooperatives (as they are correctly named), hotel-condominiums, timeshares, and planned urban developments, or PUDs. Buyers must deal with such concepts as condominium documents, homeowners associations, common and limited-common elements, maintenance assessments, and special assessments, as well as fairly complex financing and taxation issues.

In the ensuing chapters, we will explore each of these areas in depth so that you will understand exactly what you are purchasing when you buy a co-op, condo, or townhouse. You will be able to make an informed decision on your investment in real estate, rather than relying on the word of salespeople, who don't have your best interests in mind, or the advice of friends and family, who may not have the requisite knowledge, experience, or perspective to provide the correct advice for you, the individual investor.

ALL REAL ESTATE IS AN INVESTMENT

You will note that I use the term *investor*. In this book, any purchase of real property is deemed to be an investment. Too many times have people commented to me, "I bought this property to live in, not as an investment." That is wrong because it implies that the purchaser does not care about the value of the property once the purchase is made. You may purchase stocks or bonds for the dividend income, but does that mean you want the value of the shares to go down? If the value does go down, might that not affect the dividend income? It is the same with real estate. Here are three important concepts to keep in mind when considering the purchase of any property:

1. As a general rule, real estate tends to appreciate while personal

you need not sell it to raise capital; you can mortgage it. You can refinance your mortgage when the rates go down and it is advantageous to do so. Prior to lending money for a new purchase or refinancing an existing mortgage, lending institutions will appraise the property to determine its value in the marketplace. To get the most money available and at the best interest rates and terms, it is in your interest to have the values at the highest point the market will allow. We will discuss mortgages in Chapter 8 on financing.

An investment is any purchase where you have a reasonable expectation that your purchase will increase in value over time. Since real estate tends to appreciate over time (they aren't making it anymore, as Mark Twain said), a purchase of real estate falls within our definition of investment, regardless of your motives in making the purchase.

Let's test the definition. What about the purchase of an automobile? First, an automobile is personal property, so it tends to depreciate. Barring a purchase of some sort of "classic" automobile, there is no reasonable expectation on the part of a purchaser that his or her four-door sedan is going to rise in value. In fact, we know that the value of the car drops as soon as it leaves the sales parking lot. Therefore, under our definition, the purchase of a car is not an investment.

If indeed you accept that the purchase of real property represents an investment, then essentially, we are talking about making money. The bottom line is that an investment in real estate should serve your immediate needs, such as a place to live, or to rent for income, but at some point, should rise in value and yield a profit. If you, the investor, understand the nature of your real estate purchase and how the various facets of purchase, ownership, and sale operate, you will make an intelligent investment that, all things being equal, will be an enjoyable as well as profitable experience for you.

QUICK QUIZ

1. The purchase of real estate should
   a. Always be considered an investment.
   b. Only be considered an investment if it is going to be leased by the owner.
   c. Never be regarded as an investment.
   d. Never be considered an investment because it depreciates over time.

2. Which of the following is NOT an investment?
   a. A condominium
   b. A cooperative
   c. A townhouse
   d. Furniture

ANSWERS

1. (a) is the correct answer. The purchase of real estate should always be considered an investment, irrespective of the purpose of its purchase. Therefore, (b) and (c) are incorrect; (d) is incorrect because real estate tends to *appreciate* over time.

2. (d) is the correct answer. Condominiums, cooperatives, and townhouses are forms of real property. Furniture is personal property and tends to depreciate (barring the purchase of collectors' items). Therefore, under our definition of an investment, furniture is not an investment.

CHAPTER 1

As stated in the introduction, today's real estate investor is no longer limited to a few styles of private residential housing but has the opportunity to invest in a variety of residential projects. In this and subsequent chapters, we are going to explore in detail investments in condominiums, cooperatives, hotel-condominiums, timeshares, and townhouses. At the close of the book, the reader should have an understanding of each of these types of investments and the legal and economic differences they represent. Before specifically discussing each of these investment opportunities, we will take a brief look at the real estate purchase in general.

THE PURCHASE OF REAL ESTATE—TRADITIONAL AND NEW CONCEPTS IN PROPERTY OWNERSHIP

A real estate purchase traditionally has two essential components: the raw land and the improvements placed on that land. The raw land is self-explanatory. It is simply the earth upon which you walk. The crucial factor is what one does with the land. This is the second component of the discussion, the improvements added to the raw land. Improvements can take many forms.

Traditionally, land was used for farming. With the emergence of the Industrial Revolution, a new business class emerged and the nobility lost its exclusivity on land ownership. Factories were constructed, and as people came to the urban centers to work, additional housing in the form of apartment buildings were constructed. Historically, the American system of real estate is derived from the British system, which was constructed in a nation of landlords. The landowners were the nobility, and peasants or serfs worked the land and paid a tax to the landlords. Those workers were the tenants.

The landlord–tenant relationship was brought to the United States and survives to this day. However, fundamental to the culture of the United States is the concept of home ownership by every citizen who so desires. This is part of the American Dream. What has changed is the nature of what constitutes owning a home.

With the advent of condominiums, one need not buy a piece of land and build a house or a building in order to own real estate, either to live in personally or to have as income-producing property. Today, one may purchase an individual unit in a large complex and have all the advantages and, arguably, the disadvantages of both apartment living and real estate ownership.

For example, some of us, myself included, have no particular talents when it comes to home upkeep and repair. Living in a condominium provides an advantage in that it removes from the owner many of the day-to-day responsibilities of home ownership. Thus, if the lawn needs mowing, you don't have to do it. Other advantages may include the use of amenities and services. An owner of a private house may not be able to afford the luxury of a swimming pool, tennis court, gymnasium, meeting rooms, or even a golf course near his or her home. However, a condominium owner may be able to afford those luxuries because the upkeep is shared by all the owners.

This brings us to another term that you need to become familiar with prior to our entering into a more detailed analysis of real estate investments—that term is *community living*. Although you sacrifice some of the freedoms that you have with private home ownership by subjecting yourself to the rules and regulations of the condominium association, you may gain much more in terms of overall lifestyle.

COMMUNITY LIVING

In essence, when you purchase a condominium or cooperative-style investment, you are going to be living with other unit owners who made similar purchases in the same building. Your neighbors will be next to you, separated by adjoining walls, or underneath or above you, separated by floors and ceilings. No longer is your neighbor on another physically separate piece of property in a physically separate structure. Additionally, you will

fore, under this definition, community living applies not only to condominiums, but also to each type of investment discussed in this and subsequent chapters. We shall see how the application of community living affects each unit owner and why it is important to understand this concept at the onset. At this point, let's turn to the various types of investments, beginning with condominiums.

CONDOMINIUMS

Condominiums came on the scene in the 1960s and rapidly grew in popularity. They have three essential characteristics:

1. You own your individual apartment as you would a private house. It is for all legal purposes *real property*.
2. You own an undivided percentage of the common elements of the building in conjunction with the other unit owners.
3. It is governed by a board of directors that maintains the common elements and enforces the rules and regulations.

Let's take a closer look at these characteristics. The first identifies the legal status of the purchase. When you buy a condominium, you receive a deed for your apartment just as you would with a private house. Legally speaking, there is no difference. Your apartment is part of the building that constitutes the improvement of raw land. Basically, you own everything within the walls of your apartment. However, as we shall see in the chapters on condominium living, there are some exceptions. For now, it is important to understand the basic concepts.

The second characteristic indicates that you also own a proportionate share of the common elements of the raw land and the common improvements placed upon it, such as the hallways, elevators, and other areas common to the building itself. That proportionate share is usually determined based on the square footage of your unit. As it is an undivided interest, your rights in the common areas are shared with the other owners. There could be exceptions to this characteristic, which we will discuss in the chapter on purchasing your investment, so it is essential that you understand these characteristics.

Third, you are subject to state laws governing condominiums, as well as to the specific rules and regulations set out in your condominium documents. These rules govern everything from how much money you must pay the association each month, to what hours you may use the swimming pool or the common laundry facilities, to whether pets are allowed. Let's review some practical examples.

Simply put, in a condominium, if it is inside the apartment you own it and it is your responsibility. If your dishwasher breaks, you—not the building management—are responsible for getting it fixed. If a light in the common hallway goes out, the building management is responsible for replacing it, not you personally.

If the condominium rules say you may not keep a dog over 20 pounds, and your dog is 30 pounds, either Fido goes on a diet or Fido goes, regardless of the fact that he lives in your individual unit. For many people, that is a hard concept to grasp, but that is the nature of community living. You are subject to the common rules of the condominium. As already stated, there are numerous exceptions to these characteristics that you will need to be aware of. We will discuss these in greater detail in the chapter on purchasing a real estate investment, but for now, you should understand the basic concepts.

Advantages of a Condominium

Ownership of Real Estate with Apartment-Style Living. In a condominium, you are personally responsible for the interior of your unit but not the common elements such as the lawn or roof maintenance, or common amenities that are taken care of by whoever manages the common elements of the complex. You enjoy the advantages of an apartment complex while you gain equity in a real estate investment.

Increased Amenities. Unless you have a celebrity income, most people cannot afford nor have the space for swimming pools, tennis courts, health club facilities, valets, and front-desk personnel including security and, in some complexes, concierge services. But in a condominium, where many units pool their monthly assessments, such amenities are possible. Many buildings have gymnasiums, swimming pools, and all manner of services.

minium association.

You Can't Do That. You may be restricted in what you can and cannot do. For example, many condominiums have architectural committees that review a unit owner's renovation plans, and often, they have the power to disapprove them if they feel it would adversely affect the condominium. You may be restricted in terms of how many guests may stay with you in the unit, or perhaps if you have a party, how loud you may play the music. If you don't like your parking space, you may be out of luck.

COOPERATIVES

There has been much confusion between condominiums and cooperatives. Too many people have asked why it makes a difference whether you buy a cooperative or a condominium. Let me assure you that it does, legally and as an investment. The key to understanding the difference between the two is that a condominium is a real estate transaction. Your ownership is based on the legal principles of real estate law just as in the purchase of a house. In the case of a cooperative, possession is based on principles of corporate law, not real estate law.

When you purchase a cooperative, you are buying shares in a corporate entity whose assets include the building where you are going to live. It is the same as if you were to purchase shares in General Motors Corporation. The board of directors, representing the shareholders, then enters into an agreement, generally in the form of an assignment, which allows you to occupy whatever apartment is at issue for as long as you pay your required assessments. Your contract (or assignment) will also dictate what your personal responsibilities are with regard to the care and maintenance of the interior portion of the unit you are occupying. As you can see, this is a very different type of transaction from the purchase of real estate.

KEY POINT: In a cooperative, you don't actually own your apartment but rather, you own shares in a corporate entity with the contractual right to occupy your assigned unit.

Cooperatives as an Investment

If this sounds less appetizing than outright ownership of your property, as in the case of a condominium, you are correct. Cooperatives generally tend to appreciate less than, and more slowly than, condominiums. In fact, a number of cooperatives have converted to condominiums in order to improve their value in the marketplace. Yet cooperatives are still popular in such places as New York City and in France, where it is the primary method of purchase of nonrental apartments. (There are many possible reasons for this, but basically, cooperatives existed prior to condominiums.) Because condominiums do tend to have greater appreciation than cooperatives, developers and purchasers of new buildings tend to favor the condominium format.

Another problem with cooperatives is that because they basically involve a private corporate transaction, there is less federal or state government control over the boards of directors of cooperatives and, consequently, they are more powerful than their condominium counterparts. I recall seeing an episode of *Seinfeld*, where Jerry Seinfeld attempts to purchase a cooperative but is frustrated by the fact that the board of directors will not approve the sale of shares to "show-business" people. Translate *show-business people* into people of race, creed, color, national origin, or sexual preference, and discriminatory practices may abound. In fact, while great legal strides have been made in the area of antidiscrimination laws with regard to public corporations that operate in the United States and whose shares are traded publicly on the various stock exchanges, privately held corporations are often immune from those laws. And although condominium associations are also corporate entities, the boards of directors and the members of the association have little control over an individual's sale of his or her real property and are limited by state law as to what they may or may not consider in their approval process.

In addition to a generally more difficult approval process, transfer of shares in a cooperative is legally complex and therefore more expensive because fewer attorneys are comfortable working with cooperatives sales. This also contributes to the lower appreciation of cooperatives as an investment. Some people argue that it is more important to invest in affordable housing rather than continue to pay rent, even if the in

... chapter. The teaching point here is that when you are investing in a cooperative, you are not, strictly speaking, directly investing in real estate, but are investing in a corporation that owns real estate, a part of which you have a contractual or assigned right to occupy.

This discussion should not be viewed as a general attack on cooperative associations. However, perception plays an important role in the value of an investment. The *Seinfeld* episode discussed previously is an example of art imitating life. The episode was funny and relevant because people identify, or perceive that the problems Seinfeld was having purchasing a cooperative are both real and common. That perception often translates into relative value. We will revisit the issue of perception in the next chapter.

Advantages of a Cooperative

Price. Cooperatives are often less expensive than condominiums, even though they may offer similar apartments and amenities. As already indicated, this may be an attractive alternative for those wishing to make an investment in an apartment complex but at a lower cost than required for a condominium.

CAUTION: Although a cooperative may carry a less-expensive price tag, this may not mean that the monthly carrying charges are automatically less as well. Monthly maintenance is a function of effective management, the age of the building, what repairs may be required as a consequence, and many other factors that will be discussed in subsequent chapters.

Disadvantages of a Cooperative

Appreciation. Cooperatives tend to appreciate less than condominiums because of various legal and technical aspects already discussed that are inherent in the purchase of a cooperative.

Power of the Board of Directors. Because it is basically a corporation with shareholders, the rights of the residents are fundamentally based in corporate law rather than real property law. This removes many of the restrictions that limit the power of condominium boards on ownership of private property. While not totally unbridled, cooperative boards, overall, wield much more power than condominium boards.

More Difficult to Buy and Sell. Technically speaking, it is more complicated to effectuate the purchase and sale of a cooperative apartment as opposed to a condominium. In addition, it may be more difficult to find a bank that is willing to secure the financing of a cooperative as opposed to the more popular condominium, which is a purchase of real estate. The degree of difficulty may affect the rate as well.

The Hotel-Condominium

The hotel-condominium is the newest innovation in real estate investing. It is, generally speaking, an investment for people who wish to purchase real estate for both appreciation value and income, but not for personal residence. From the standpoint of the investor, it operates in the following manner. The investor purchases an apartment in a building as one would a normal condominium. The purchaser receives a deed and is the owner of that particular unit. Along with the deed, the purchaser will also receive a set of condominium documents outlining rights and liabilities with regard to the ownership of the unit. There will also be a board of directors, which is elected. However, the basic premise of the hotel-condominium is, as the name suggests, that it operates as a hotel, rather than a personal residence.

Looks Like a Hotel, Feels Like a Hotel, But It's a Condominium

Many hotels are, in actuality, hotel-condominiums, and the guests do not know the difference. Thus, along with the normal set of condominium documents, the purchaser gets a second set of documents that states, in detail, the nature of the relationship between the hotel operation and the owners. These must be examined by the purchaser with great care. In most cases, the developer will have entered into a multiyear contract with a hotel operator such as Doubletree or Hilton to run the hotel operation. The hotel operation's portion of the condominium documents describes what rights the purchaser has with regard to the hotel operation, usually according to a *hotel plan*. The hotel plan is the agreement between the hotel operator and the individual unit owners concerning the rights and responsibilities related to the hotel operation. The hotel plans vary, so it is important to understand exactly what type of plan is in effect for the development that you are considering.

For example, since a key to successful hotel operations is the availability of rooms to rent to guests, the documents may require the purchaser to place his or her unit in the hotel plan for a certain period of time. Other variations to a hotel plan may allow the purchaser to live in the unit, but if they wish to lease it, they may only do so under the hotel plan. Other operations freely allow the purchaser to lease his or her own unit on their own or under the hotel plan as they see fit or to have unlimited personal use.

How a Hotel-Condominium Operates for the Purchaser

We once had a client who wished to purchase an oceanfront property in the Miami Beach area; however, she gave us the following constraint: She did not live in the United States and would only be using the property two or three weeks out of the year at the most. Therefore, she wanted it leased except during those infrequent visits to the United States, when she required that it be available for her personal use. Those visits were not preplanned and were totally discretionary as her travel itinerary and schedule mandated.

This constraint presented a difficult problem. The unit had to be available to the client for three nonconsecutive weeks of the year. Most condominiums have leasing restrictions that generally require the owner to lease his or her unit for a specific number of months and only for a specific number of times per year. That being the case, it would be difficult, if not impossible, to guarantee that the client's unit would be available for three, nonconsecutive, and possibly impromptu visits during the year. "We're sorry Mr. or Ms. Tenant, but the owner wants her unit for a week so you have to leave," is obviously not a viable scenario.

The answer was a hotel-condominium. After a bit of research, we found an oceanfront hotel-condominium that met her constraints. The hotel had the following requirements, all of which were no problem for this particular investor:

1.   The purchaser did not have to put the unit in the hotel plan, but if he or she chose to do so, it had to be in the peak hotel season for a period of not less than three months.

2.   The purchaser could remove the apartment from the plan but would not be entitled to hotel-style services such as room, maid service, or even parking services.

3.   If the purchaser chose to keep the apartment on the hotel plan but wished to use it during a period that the unit was occupied by a guest, the hotel would provide a similar apartment to the owner but the owner would not be entitled to hotel services.

Our research indicated that the hotel was in operation for about three years and had broken even the last fiscal year. It estimated that it would operate at a profit in the next year. This, we discovered, was not unusual for a new hotel. In addition, and more importantly for the purchaser, the apartments had appreciated in value, due mainly to the overall appreciation of property in that particular area. Further, at the current occupancy level (the average amount of time the hotel rooms are rented over the course of the year), if the investor could pay a 50 percent down payment and obtain a mortgage for the other 50 percent, her share of the rental proceeds from the hotel operation would cover the maintenance and fees as well as the mortgage payment—provided that the purchaser kept the apartment on the hotel program for 11 of the 12 months of the year.

The unit was sold furnished to hotel standards, and it was estimated that the purchaser would not have to upgrade for about three years. In addition, there was insurance available in case of a guest damaging the furniture, which the hotel partially absorbed. Finally, this particular hotel divided the profits based on the totality of that particular category of apartments (i.e., one-bedroom units) rented quarterly rather than the specific apartment itself. Therefore, the amount of income made by the investor was not strictly dependent on that specific apartment being rented.

Again, in a hotel-condominium situation, it is crucial that the investor understand the hotel plan. Unless you know for a fact that your particular apartment will always be rented, which is often difficult to gauge, it is better to be in a situation where your income is based on an overall performance of an apartment category. Thus, even if your apartment is vacant, you still earn income if other apartments in your same category are rented. The odds in your favor are far greater under this type of plan. For our

purchase a condominium for which you receive a deed and a set of condominium documents that state your rights as a property owner.

2. You receive a second set of condominium documents that indicate your rights as they apply to the hotel operation. These may contain such details as use of the amenities, furnishing and upgrades of the unit, division of costs, and information on the hotel operator as well as the terms and conditions of his or her contract with the developer and subsequent association.

Hotel-condominiums are a relatively new concept and are still developing conceptually, based on the originality of the developers. For example, there is a new development that is part condominium and part hotel-condominium. The first 25 floors are hotel-condominium and the second 25 floors are pure condominium. To make the scenario a bit more complex, the condominium documents state that the hotel operator owns the amenities.

This harkens back to the recreation lease system where a purchaser acquired the rights to the apartment but not the common element amenities such as the swimming pool or tennis courts. These were owned by a separate company that charged the unit owners rent for their use. The rent was a mandatory fee included in the monthly maintenance assessment of the unit owners. Some states have made recreation leases illegal or the associations have bought out these leases on their own. In the scenario just described, what happens if the hotel operator holds a pool party for the hotel guests only and does not allow the condominium owners to use the swimming pool, health club, or the gymnasium?

Condominium documents tend to be general in nature and don't always provide clear answers to specific situations. Sometimes, there is no specific answer and the problem must be resolved by either litigation or legislation. Litigation can be costly and frustrating and not something you want to be involved with if you can at all help it. Therefore, if you can spot an issue first and get a satisfactory resolution before you make the purchase, you are much better off.

Another hotel-condominium document stated that owners who do not place their units on the hotel plan but, rather, lease them on their own, cannot have their tenants use any of the hotel amenities. In a condominium, legally, when an owner leases a unit, the right to use the common elements, including the use of the amenities, shifts from the owner to the tenant during the term of the lease. In this case, the hotel operator is attempting to restrict that law. Can such a restriction legally be imposed on an owner, or is that an unconstitutional limitation, or *alienation* of an owner's property rights? The courts will probably have to rule on this issue, and there is currently at least one case on point in the court system in Florida.

In Chapter 4, "Buying Directly from a Developer," we will discuss what you can do if these issues arise. For the moment, if you are thinking of investing in a hotel-condominium or a condominium that contains hotel-condominium units, you should be sensitive to these types of issues. Regardless of the possible pitfalls, hotel-condominiums are an exciting new twist to the condominium real estate market and deserve careful consideration.

Advantages of a Hotel-Condominium

Basic Concept Is Income Production. The hotel-condominium is designed to produce income for the purchaser rather than be available for personal use. A successful hotel-condominium can carry itself in terms of costs and produce a profit as well.

Disadvantages of a Hotel-Condominium

Limited Use by the Owner. For the same reason it produces income for the buyer, it means that the owner will not be able to use it except for limited periods of time.

Limited Use of the Amenities. With a hotel-condominium, the owner may not receive a permanent parking space or be able to use the amenities while the unit is under the hotel plan.

Limited Ability to Lease the Unit. The condo documents may limit the owner's rights to lease the unit on his or her own and without entering into the hotel plan.

investment. Conceptually, it was a great idea that was poorly implemented.

The basic premise was, if you could sell an apartment once, why not sell it twice or even 52 times? So a developer would buy a hotel, refurbish it, staff it with personnel so it operated like a hotel or motel, and then literally divide each unit into weekly increments for sale. Each purchaser, for a fraction of the cost, could buy as little as one week of exclusive use of the apartment, for which he or she received a deed. Since the purchaser was buying only a week of use, that purchaser owned $1/52$ of undivided, exclusive use of the condominium. Of course, the purchase price was a fraction of the cost of a full ownership, and so it theoretically should have had mass appeal.

Consider you have a job that allows you two weeks of vacation around the same time each year. In addition, budget constraints would prohibit going to a resort of equal quality to the timeshare resort. However, with the timeshare, the purchase price was not prohibitive and the carrying costs were equally small, for the same reason. Plus, your $1/52$ was ownership of real property that could be sold, presumably at a profit in the future. Had the developers and their marketing people stopped there, the concept would probably have been a modest success with no major repercussions. But that is not the way things work in a free-market economy. If you have an idea, you maximize it, and that is exactly what happened with timeshare. The timeshare developers must have thought, "What a great idea we have—how can we really push it to the hilt?" What they came up with was a logical continuation of the timeshare concept and it was, ultimately, its downfall.

They decided, "If we can sell each unit of a 50-unit motel 52 times, why not unite all of the timeshare resorts into one giant worldwide network and allow the owners to trade resorts? Just think, you could buy a week of timeshare in North Podunk and vacation in the Greek Isles. We could sell timeshare globally, the profits would be enormous."

That is exactly what the timeshare developers set out to do. Central networks were created with the idea of coordinating the trading of time-shares (for a small administrative fee) by and between members of the time-share networks. In theory, it was an exciting idea and initially it caught on, but there were problems.

Problems with Timeshares

The first problem was that there were few legislative controls on timeshare, and as a result, there were misrepresentations in the marketing of time-shares. High-pressure tactics were used to market and sell the product with-out fully disclosing what was involved. For example, if you purchased two very cheap weeks in North Podunk in the winter, it was unlikely that anyone would want to trade their own timeshare in the Greek Isles to visit yours, making it highly unlikely that you could ever exercise your right to trade. Further, even if your exchange program did allow you to trade for the Greek Isles, the central networks themselves were poorly organized and incapable of coordinating all the exchange requests. Thus, an exchange often required reserving a year or more in advance and, more often than not, travelers who were able to exchange would arrive at their destination only to find another couple already occupying the property. In other more severe cases, the property advertised under the exchange program bore little resemblance to the brochures offered in the exchange program and were totally unsuitable.

Another problem, as it turned out, was that timeshare was ultimately a poor real estate investment. Because there were so many "weeks" being sold, along with new properties being built or older properties being reno-vated, the laws of supply and demand eventually took hold. When purchas-ers sought to sell their timeshare holdings, there was little or no demand for them. In addition, because timeshare property was on the fringe of normal real estate transactions, there were few brokers who dealt in it. Eventually, special sales groups were set up to coordinate sales of timeshare properties, but by that time, the supply far exceeded the demand and sales were few, far between, and not profitable.

Still another problem with timeshare was that underneath all the hype, it was still a condominium. As we learned, condominiums are run like corporations with boards of directors who are charged with the responsibility of collecting each unit owner's assessments, which are used to maintain and operate the properties. Because the investments were relatively small and there were so many purchasers for each unit, keeping track of each individual owner was an administrative nightmare.

to the near impossible administrative burden of locating literally thousands of holders of timeshare deeds to obtain releases to the property or otherwise comply with state notice requirements involving the property.

Timeshare Today

Today, timeshare sales are regulated and subject to state laws. Full disclosure of every aspect of the timeshare operation is generally required, condominium documents are issued, and there is a right of rescission or *cooling-off period* (usually three to ten days, depending on state law) where the purchaser can back out. In spite of its dubious origins, there are holders of timeshares who are happy with their purchases and use their exchange programs, which are now vastly improved. However, the stigma of timeshare still exists, and as an investment, it has never met its full potential. Nevertheless, the concept continues to evolve.

Many large hotel chains, eager to expand their empires, have vacation plans that essentially have their roots in the timeshare concept. Oddly enough, they don't want to be associated with timeshare, both for certain legal reasons, but more likely, to avoid the historical stigma. During a recent stay at a hotel that was also marketing its vacation club plan, my wife and I were approached by a salesperson. The first words out of the salesperson's mouth were, "It isn't timeshare." While these vacation plans vary from purchasing shares in vacation plans, to incremental time in hotel-style property, to purchase of points that may be redeemed at the hotel operators' resorts, the concept of incremental sales in an exchange program has its roots in timeshare.

Vacation plans are beyond the scope of this book, but as a learning point, it should be noted that a purchase of any type of vacation plan not accompanied by a deed of ownership in a property is not a purchase of real estate. Recall that the basic premise of this book is that all real estate purchases are an investment of your capital and credit.

Advantages of Timeshare

Small Investment. A week or two of timeshare in a resort is still an investment in real estate, but with a small dollar amount.

Use of Other Timeshares. Most timeshare plans offer trades or *exchange programs* for other timeshare facilities worldwide, thus affording the investor an opportunity to trade two weeks in the United States for a facility somewhere around the globe.

Disadvantages of Timeshare

Difficult to Resell. Traditionally, timeshare investments were difficult to resell, mainly due to the high amount of supply. Also, exchange programs were not well operated. Today, the exchange systems have improved and many people are satisfied with their investment in timeshare, and there are agencies that specialize in the sale of timeshare properties. However, they still remain a difficult sale with limited appreciation.

TOWNHOUSES

Townhouses are simply clusters of private houses that are attached by common walls. They are also known by the rather anachronistic term *semidetached* homes. Townhouses enjoy some of the attributes of a house in terms of size. A townhouse may encompass three or more floors and have a small private yard as well as common-element grounds that are maintained by an association. Generally, the homeowners association documents will determine what are common elements and what are the responsibilities of the homeowner.

Community Associations

In this book, we are going to be concerned with those townhouses that are part of and governed by a residential homeowners association and whose residents are subject to the constraints of community homeowners associations. Community homeowners associations are the common thread of condominiums, cooperatives, hotel-condominiums, timeshares and townhouses.

In some states, the term *PUD* is used. PUD stands for *planned urban development*. They are communities that may contain private houses, townhouses, condominiums, or a combination of each, and are generally governed by a homeowners association. However, the specific laws for

than a condominium, which is in reality just an apartment. A townhouse may have several levels and possibly a private garage and private yard. Some townhouses have large private decks, as opposed to smaller terraces found in many condominiums.

Amenities. Because it is not a private home but part of a homeowners association, some townhouse communities may offer common-element amenities such as tennis and golf or community swimming pools.

Less Expensive than a Private Home. Generally speaking, townhouses can be more affordable than a private home or many condominiums. Like a condominium, there is going to be less for the owner to be concerned with such as lawn care.

Disadvantages of a Townhouse

Privacy. Unlike a private home, your neighbor is living in the townhouse next door to you, which is attached by a common wall. Poor or improper sound insulation and a noisy neighbor can make for difficult living conditions. Because townhouses tend to have more aspects of private home living, associations are less likely to enforce rules and regulations than in an apartment complex, where close proximity of numerous owners makes it more imperative that rules and regulations are strictly enforced.

SUMMARY

By now, you should understand and appreciate the differences between condominiums, cooperatives, hotel-condominiums, timeshares, and townhouses. Table 1-1 presents the differences in an easy-to-read chart for your reference here and in future chapters. In the next chapter, we will debunk

Table 1-1. Comparison of Real Estate Investments.

	Condo	Co-op	Townhouse	Timeshare	Hotel-Condo
Investment Category	Real estate	Corporate shares	Real estate	Real estate	Real estate
Type of Ownership	Individual unit ownership by deed	Shares in corporation with assignment of unit	Individual ownership by deed	Individual ownership of limited time period by deed	Individual ownership by deed
Governing Documents	Condo documents	Corporate charter	Homeowners association documents	Condo documents	Separate condo documents for hotel operation and unit ownership
Leasing of Property	Possible lease restrictions. Board approval is often required.	Possible lease restrictions. Board approval is often required.	Possible lease restrictions. Board approval may be required, but there is generally less interference by board.	Not conducive to leasing.	Leasing by owner may be severely limited. Careful reading of both sets of condo documents is strongly suggested.
Power of Board of Directors	Association boards have less control over purchase and sale.	Association boards have greater powers over purchase and sale.	Association boards tend to be less powerful and interfere less in purchase and sale.	Association boards tend to rely heavily on management companies. There is little interference in purchase and sale.	Association boards tend to rely on the hotel management group and do not interfere in the operation of the property. There is little interference in purchase and sale.

Financing	Mortgages are generally not an issue. They are based on the credit-worthiness of the applicant and appraisal of the property.	Financing of cooperative units is more difficult to obtain and requires specialized financing.	Mortgages are g-enerally not an issue. They are based on the credit-worthiness of the applicant and ap-praisal of the prop-erty.	Fin tim is n obt ofte ran;	ng is mostly the same as condomin- t may carry remium for hotel- Not all lend- itutions will rtgages on ondos.
Investment Potential	Property tends to appreciate in value in accordance with real estate trends.	Purchase may ap-preciate in value, but not usually as well as a condo.	Property tends to appreciate in value in accordance with real estate trends.	Tim prec on s estal excl open low	y usually ap- s in accor- ith real ends, but tion may be by how hotel oper- how much the unit s.

one of the great myths of real estate, after which we will learn how developers create and define a real estate project and designate it to be a condominium or cooperative. We will also explore the ramifications of purchasing a property directly from a developer. What should you, the purchaser be aware of? What should you expect from a sales staff? More importantly, how should you best negotiate for your purchase?

CHAPTER 2

Searching for a condo, co-op, or townhouse (as well as a hotel-condominium or timeshare), like any other task, requires preparation. Some of the factors you may wish to consider before hitting the streets include an honest assessment of how much you can afford to invest in your purchase and how much per month you can spend carrying it. You may wish to check your credit history to see if there is any incorrect information that might not only be embarrassing, but could also either raise your mortgage rate or cause you to be denied when the time comes for you to apply for a loan. Some real estate experts recommend getting a prequalification letter from your lending institution. We will talk more about this later in this chapter. You may also wish to find a qualified real estate broker.

How Much Can You Afford?

This is the big question, and there is no exact answer because there are a great number of variables that may apply. For example, banks will calculate your income and expenses and arrive at a conclusion as to what they consider you can afford. Banks and financial advisers love specific numbers and rules.

One of many rules of thumb is that you should spend no more than 25 percent of your gross income on housing. The problem is that income and expenses vary greatly, based on your needs and priorities, or external factors that you cannot control. To buy the condo of your dreams you may sacrifice that new car, forgo your annual vacation, or take an extra job. Another consideration is whether the property will generate income. If you plan to lease your property while it appreciates, that could improve your ability to carry the property. Those are factors that you can control. But what if you lose your job or the real estate market changes or the tenant moves out or the economy deteriorates? What happens if there are unforeseen expenses such as a roof repair to the building for which you receive a special assessment? How long can you carry the property during bad times?

Our general advice is you should have enough savings to carry the property at least six months if things go bad. In real estate, in the long term, as we stress, property does tend to rebound and appreciate. You have to be able to hold out.

If you want to get a rough evaluation of what lenders think you can afford, get a prequalification letter from your local bank and see what they say. Built into the bank's prequalification software are averages between percentages of your gross income and net income to provide a conclusion as to how much you can afford to spend on a mortgage. You must take the prequalification recommendation with a grain of salt.

KEY POINT: Most people have an instinct for what they can and cannot afford without applying an arbitrary percentage of income and expense as a determining factor. For example, most people know what kind of car they can afford, and if they want better, what adjustments to their lifestyle they are willing to make. We have a friend who has been driving the same car for 25 years, hasn't stayed in a hotel in at least 15 years, hardly goes to a mall, and never eats at a restaurant. But she owns the most beautiful beach house imaginable, as well as a large and expensive condominium in the city. She isn't rich. Most of her disposable income goes into maintaining her properties.

Rules of thumb are very inexact and should be viewed with caution. Also, when you make a real estate investment, you will need to know not only the price, but also the monthly carrying charges, the real estate taxes, possible special assessments, and other costs. In other words, using the 25 percent rule, if you do your own calculation, you may be right at that point of insufficient cash to continue to live as you do now. By contrast, you may be well under what you are already paying for rent and comfortable with spending. Does that mean it is safe to make the purchase? Perhaps not. That is why you need to be wary of rigid economic rules. At this early point in your search, you should be concerned with having a general price

the term *prequalification* because it doesn't qualify you for anything, and there is no commitment by the lending institution to honor it. However, the prequalification letter does serve a number of useful purposes. It does give you a rough idea of how much the lending institution considers you can borrow, other things being equal. As we will see in more detail in Chapter 8 on financing, unlike borrowing a car, where the lending institution does not care what kind of car you buy, as long as it calculates that you can repay the loan, in real estate, the bank will also look at the property you are purchasing.

Also, some sellers will want to see a prequalification letter before allowing you to submit a contract on their property. Their fear is that you won't qualify for the loan and meanwhile, their property is off the market. However, sellers often fail to realize that if their property is priced too high, the buyer can be prequalified for the loan amount and banks will still deny the loan because the property won't appraise. We will discuss this in greater detail later in the book, however for now, understand the limits of a pre-qualification letter.

Checking Your Credit

Experts love to wax prolific on this subject because it is an integral part of securing a loan. How good your credit rating is will determine if you can secure a loan and at what rate. We will discuss the specifics of credit in Chapter 8, but at this early point in the process, you should at least know your credit score and history and try to correct any mistakes. There are three credit-reporting agencies that you may contact and that much furnish you your credit information:

1. Equifax
   P.O. Box 740241
   Atlanta, GA 30374-0241
   1-800-685-1111
   www.equifax.com

2. Experian (formerly TRW)
   P.O. Box 2104
   Allen, TX 65013-2104
   1-888-397-3742
   www.experian.com

3. Trans Union
   P.O. Box 390
   Springfield, PA 19064-0390
   1-800-916-8800
   www.transunion.com

Your credit score, also known as the *Fair Isaac Corp*, or *FICO*, is the score that lenders use to determine if you are eligible for a loan and at what interest rate. The higher the score, the better the terms and conditions of your loan. The score is based on your past credit history, mainly whether you pay your bills on time and have any defaults on prior obligations such as credit cards or other loans. Your credit history will also show your other debts, which tells the bank what your liabilities are. The longer the credit history, the better your chances of getting a loan. Credit scores less than 500 will probably result in your being denied a loan. A good credit score is anywhere around 680 and above. Over 720 will generally get you the best available rates.

BUYER'S TIP: Checking your credit is probably the most important thing you should do before beginning your search. If you have bad credit, it will severely limit your ability to secure a loan, and it will be worth your while to improve or cure your credit first before starting your search for a property.

WISH LISTS

When I joined the Air Force, my fellow officers and I were given a wish list to fill in as to what bases we wanted to be stationed at. Of course, I picked the ones near beaches or in Europe. By pure luck, I got a great base, but most of my friends didn't even get close to what they wanted. That's why they called it a *wish list*. However, when you are determining what property to look for, there are certain considerations to factor in before you begin your search, because it will save you time:

6. Whether you require a guest room or extra room for a house-keeper or nanny

7. Rules regarding the decorating of your unit

8. Ability to lease the property

9. Ability to resell the property

BUYER'S TIP: Your search for property should be based on your real-world needs, not some fantasy presented by a developer or a sales pitch from the seller or seller's representative. Try to have a clear picture of what you require from your investment before you begin your search.

PROFESSIONAL HELP: REAL ESTATE BROKERS

You may wish to search for your home without the use of a real estate broker. However, a knowledgeable real estate professional is not only an invaluable research tool, but can cut your time in finding a suitable project.

Real estate brokers in the United States are generally licensed professionals who are subject to state and, sometimes, federal laws. Just as there are good lawyers, good accountants, and good doctors, there are good real estate brokers who know their profession and work and act on behalf of the client. They bring to the table an expertise and perspective that the layperson does not generally have, although when it comes to real estate, a great many laypeople think that they are experts. A good real estate broker knows his or her area and the market conditions, and will often negotiate a better deal for you than you could personally do. In addition, brokers can offer assistance with documents such as contracts and can offer some assistance in securing financing. Many brokers have mortgage broker's licenses as well, while others may have connections in the industry.

What to Look For

Ideally, an agent should be a *Realtor*. Realtors are members of the National Association of Realtors (NAR) and their local real estate boards. They are governed by a code of professional ethics and have resources such as computerized listing services from which they can obtain various types of information that will help you determine what properties are available and if the prices are reasonable. Some Realtors are familiar with the local boards of buildings and developers. They may have better information on the properties you are interested in and which you would not be able to know on your own.

Broker Interview Questions

Here are three questions you may wish to ask prospective agents:

1. *Who pays the commission?* The seller does 99 percent of the time.

2. *Who does the broker represent?* A broker may represent you and the seller, and this is not considered a conflict of interest. Some states require the broker to disclose at the onset his or her fiduciary duties (duties of trust and loyalty). If a broker represents the seller, it does not mean you should look for another broker. Realtors have a fiduciary duty to all parties they represent to act honestly and in each party's best interest. This is common practice.

3. *How many years of experience does the broker have in this area?* Being new to the business does not necessarily mean the Realtor is not qualified, just as having years of experience does not necessarily mean that the Realtor is a good performer. However, real estate is a competitive field, Realtors gain knowledge with experience, and poor performers will often get sifted out. Years of success in California may not translate to success in south Florida or New York, or years of experience selling houses may not translate into being an effective condominium expert. The best combination is years of experience in the location and type of property you are dealing with.

HITTING THE STREETS

What should you take into consideration when looking to buy a condo, co-op, townhouse, hotel-condo, or timeshare? As we have noted, and will

"location, location, location" as the key factor in any consideration of a real estate purchase. So popular and prevalent is the phrase that it has become a universal maxim of real estate. However, it is important to understand the limits of this phrase and to keep it in perspective when selecting a property. Using location as the sole factor in determining the suitability of a real estate purchase can lead to less-than-ideal choices. What will be illustrated in this chapter, is that *location, location, location* should not be the sole and determining factor in any investment in real estate, and certainly not in condominiums, cooperatives, and townhouses.

First, let's consider the meaning of the term *location*. A basic definition of location is a general or specific point where a person or thing is situated. For example, "John is standing on 5th Avenue and 52nd Street." "The condominium is located in Miami Beach." Those are locations, but do they tell you anything about 5th Avenue and 52nd Street or Miami Beach? Would you buy a condominium from a salesperson based solely on that information? Obviously not. Thus, by definition, location is not much more than a point on a map.

LOCATION REALLY MEANS AREA

When salespeople emphasize *location,* they are really talking about the proximity of a property to other factors within a given area. What sort of factors might one consider important to have nearby? The classic examples of relevant factors are proximity to good schools, transportation, recreational facilities, shopping and commercial centers, parking facilities, and houses of worship. Already, you can see that what we are concerned with is the overall area where the potential real estate investment is located. The term *location* is therefore too limited in scope. But is it enough to change "location, location, location" to "area, area, area"? The answer is no. Aside from the fact that "location, location, location" is a lot catchier than "area, area, area," even the broader conceptual scope of an area, as opposed to a location, is far from what is necessary to protect a purchaser from an inappropriate purchase.

Area Checklist

There are at least six factors to consider in area research:

1. How close is the property to roads and public transportation?
2. How close is the property to shopping and entertainment and houses of worship?
3. Is the area generally considered residential or commercial? (This may be a perception, which we will discuss shortly.)
4. How close is the property to schools?
5. How close is the property to medical and religious and banking institutions?
6. Is the surrounding area relatively safe in terms of crime? Can you walk in the neighborhood at night? (This may be a perception as well.)

In addition to area, two other factors should be evaluated: perception and economics. Therefore, for *location, location, location,* I'm going to substitute my own phrase: *area, perception, and economics*—or A.P.E., for those of you who love acronyms. As I explain these factors more fully, I will present three scenarios and examples to illustrate the important point I am making here about evaluating a property. In each of the scenarios, the principle of location was insufficient to make the best purchase.

> ## Scenario 1: Real Estate and the City
>
> The first scenario involves a purchase my wife and I made many years ago. It was in a city in Europe that I was not totally familiar with, but that we loved and where we had always dreamed of owning property. The location was directly in the city center. The area was in close proximity to all forms of public transportation.

It was walking distance to the local and national trains and bus service and was 15 minutes to the international airport by car. Recreational facilities included, also within walking distance, several movie houses, theaters, and concert halls, a plethora of restau

that the city center was not considered a highly desirable area to live by the local residents, but I didn't listen. The location was too perfect. After a few years, the economy changed and the real estate market was hit hard. However, the market recovered quickly— except for the city center, where we had made our purchase. Eventually, we sold the property and we did make a profit, but it was far from what we had originally projected. Based on "location, location, location" or even my expanded terminology of "area, area, area," our purchase should have been solid gold. What went wrong? What had I failed to consider?

Perceptions—The Second Key Consideration

In the example just given, we considered location as the primary factor, but my perspective was wrong. I was raised in New York City. My perspective was based on those real estate norms. In short, we equated the city center in the European city to that of New York City and specifically, midtown Manhattan, where property, with rare exceptions, was always at a premium. To me, success equated to living midtown-Manhattan style. What I failed to appreciate, and what my wife understood, was that this was not the perspective of the residents of that European city. To them, the midtown, or city center, is a place where you work or shop, play, or even send your kids to school, but not live. Also, residents of that city did not particularly understand the concept of condominium living. They traditionally lived in private houses or townhouses, but not in condominiums.

The perceptions were so strong that even during the period where the economy was very strong and the real estate market reacted accordingly with a surge of activity in the city center, it could not withstand the earlier downturn. Thus, even when the market recovered, the city center was the last to come around and never did fully regain that initial momentum because the primary purchasers, actual residents, did not want to live in the city center. Eventually, we sold our apartment to a young professional who did wish to be able to walk to work. We sold at a profit but our investment did not reach the potential we had anticipated.

KEY POINT: While analysis of the area was important, it was not the sole factor that had to be considered. When buying residential real estate, you have to consider the merits of the location, but you also have to consider the perceptions of others about that area.

Gauging Perceptions

How do you, the potential investor, investigate perceptions? Perceptions are intangibles. You can't quantify them as you can the proximity of a building to a shopping center or bus station. Yet, your major weapon in real estate investing is research. You can draw certain conclusions as to perceptions.

In the first scenario, my wife lived and studied in the European city and knew and understood the people. It was my enthusiasm to live in a Manhattan-style apartment (in fact, that was how it was marketed) and her desire to please me that prevented us from making a different purchase. I suppose that a secondary lesson is to listen to your spouse, especially if she knows what she (or he, of course) is talking about. However, since this is a book on successful real estate investing and not successful marriages, we won't further pursue this particular point.

Therefore, if you want to gauge the perceptions of the people who live in the area, speak to them. Don't be shy. This is also an advantage of engaging a knowledgeable real estate broker who knows the area. They should be able to help you in understanding the perceptions of the people in the area. This is not to say that you should accost people in the street and conduct impromptu interviews, but in the course of conversations with friends or acquaintances who live in the area, ask certain relevant questions and note their responses. For example, friends of ours who were lifetime residents were surprised that we were considering living "downtown," as it were. Our European attorney specifically advised us of the risks involved. But I didn't listen. My perception of what I was purchasing was the equivalent of a midtown-Manhattan apartment, and to this day, I still can't shake that image.

Questions such as, "How do you feel about the new construction in the city?" can assist in gauging the perceptions of the local residents. If they are planning to invest in real estate. You are trying to understand how the local residents perceive the area you are contemplating investing in and the type of investment you are planning to make. That is all. Further, asking the locals about an area is not a forum for them to air any individual prejudices based upon race, creed, color or national origin. That is not relevant to your research nor should it be.

Miami Dice—A Case in Point

Let's look at an example closer to home, specifically, my home—Miami, Florida. As I mentioned earlier, I was raised in the New York City metropolitan area, while my wife grew up in California and eventually South America and Europe. But we have both lived in the Miami area for many years. Our perception of the city of Miami is strictly a commercial area that shuts down after 5:00 P.M. That has pretty much been the perception of most people who live in south Florida.

As of this writing, developers have begun a massive building campaign of large-scale luxury condominiums in what is the downtown center of the city of Miami. The south Florida real estate market is strong, and there has been the initial spurt of activity in the purchase of units of these condominium apartments. A significant number of purchasers are investors who will not occupy the units but will plan to resell them or lease them. Another portion are younger professionals who work in the city and want to live closer to their jobs and avoid heavy rush-hour traffic. Another segment represents foreign (principally Latin) business people who come to Miami strictly to conduct their affairs in the city of Miami. However, Miami is not a very large city and area employees and foreign business people are insufficient to absorb all of the construction. In order to be successful in the long term, developers must create the perception that downtown Miami will be a choice residential area. Are they rolling the dice? Sure they are, but the payoff could be monumental, and a new and vibrant residential area could be created.

Researching Perceptions

Another way to learn about perceptions is to study the history of the area you are considering. A visit to the local library or bookstore can be an important avenue of research into the proper perception of an area. For example, there are dozens of guidebooks, photo journals, and other similar works on the history of Miami and its famous beaches. A careful reading will tell you that from its earliest days in the late 1800s, real estate land sales and development concentrated on the beaches and not the city of Miami. When developers began to build residential housing in the form of condominiums, they began their development on the beach. While developers did have to overcome the perception that Miami Beach was strictly a tourist playground, there had already been precedence of people residing in the area, and high rises in the form of hotels and rental apartments were the norm.

It was not a great stretch to sell the idea that if an area was good enough to play in, paying hotel rates or renting an apartment, it was even better to own your own apartment where you spent your vacations. It worked so well that for a period of time, Miami Beach's playground image gave way to Miami Beach being considered as a giant retirement village or high-rise condominium filled with older people who purchased apartments in a great climate and where they had enjoyed their vacation time in their younger days. Oddly enough, television shows such as *Miami Vice* helped restore the image of Miami and the beaches as an exciting, albeit slightly dangerous playground. Worldwide, many people still perceive Miami and its beaches based on a television show that was made more than 20 years ago.

Changing Perceptions: What Happens in Vegas May No Longer Stay in Vegas

Another city in the United States that has undergone a change in image is that of Las Vegas, Nevada. Historically, Las Vegas was a desert town created as a gambling resort. It developed into the gambling capital of the world. In addition, since prostitution was more or less legal, Las Vegas was the sin city playground of the United States. However, with other cities legalizing gambling and increased competition in the tourism industry worldwide, general tourism to Las Vegas began to decrease.

To restore its status in the tourism industry, Las Vegas began to change its own image to a more family-oriented playground so it would not be

change in perception of an area will be successful in terms of condominium real estate development. Of course, true to its roots, the "what happens in Las Vegas stays in Las Vegas" advertising campaign still hints at it being an adult playground, but certainly with a more tongue-in-cheek attitude.

In chapters 4 and 5, we will explore the topics of purchasing directly from developers and purchasing resales, but for now, understand that there are other factors besides location that govern real estate investments. Thus far, we have looked at the area in general and the perceptions others have of that area. Now we'll look at the third consideration, that of economics.

THE THIRD CONSIDERATION—ECONOMICS

Economics is a very broad area. It involves study of one's personal finances, external factors such as financing rates and terms, and the property costs itself, its market price and value, and management and carrying costs of the apartment. The latter two areas will be discussed in detail in chapters 4, 5, and 8 on purchasing and financing. For now, we will look at the third aspect to illustrate the limitations of considering only location.

Scenario 2: Three of a Kind?

In the second scenario, three buildings were all located within one block of each other. They were all oceanfront properties across the street from essential services such as shopping, banking, and medical services. Schools were nearby, as were a sufficient variety of houses of worship to accommodate the major world religions. Each building had similar apartments and amenities, although owners in buildings A and C paid less in maintenance assessments than building B. However, building B was a smaller building with more personalized services than the other two much larger buildings. In terms of resale profits for their purchasers, buildings A and C outperformed building B both in price per square foot resale and length of time it took to effectuate a sale. If all were in the same location, why should this happen? Obviously there must have been other considerations? What were they?

Compare and Contrast

Here we see three similar properties in the same location. However, we are told that condominium B sells for less than the other two. To account for this, there must be some other factors at work other than location. Using our A.P.E. system, we already know the area and perceptions are the same. Therefore, there has to be some third factor affecting the price of the investment. The answer should thus lie in the economic consideration.

We are told that the maintenance in building B is more than that of the other two. That is the relevant clue. The smaller building has fewer apartments to support it, although every building has certain fixed costs regardless of size. Fixed costs include management fees, insurance policies, maintenance contracts for elevators, common-element air conditioner systems, and landscaping and refuse collection. These are fairly standardized regardless of the size of the building. Building B also has an in-house labor force, including a full time engineer, an assistant, and two laborers and three full-time cleaners. All had high-end salaries and benefits. The building also boasts 24-hour in-house security, including one front desk concierge and a security guard at all times. The building maintains two valets on a 24-hour basis, along with a pool attendant and assistant.

Although buildings A and C have similar services and amenities, those buildings have roughly two and one half times the amount of units to divide up maintenance costs.

CONSIDER THIS: Although the residents of building B have complained about the higher maintenance payments, they have been unwilling to entertain any changes related to cost cutting. However, when an owner wishes to sell his or her unit, the higher maintenance costs have a chilling effect on potential buyers. The majority of buyers choose apartments in buildings A and C, which are similar but have less carrying charges. Those buyers who wish to sell their units have to lower the sales price to compensate for the higher monthly maintenance costs. As a result, building B units do not sell as fast or command as high a price as units in buildings A and C.

In later chapters, we will explore in greater detail how you ... the in

near his job. The community was also close to the best public schools in the state and all forms of shopping, but not much public transportation. However, the community had a large swimming pool and tennis courts for its residents and was well maintained. The client was the second owner of the property. The state's economy was booming and the real estate market was strong. After several years, the client decided to sell his house and return to Florida. Although he made a profit, it did not perform as well as expected. Why? Based on the principle of location, location, location, it should have done magnificently. What had he failed to consider?

In this situation, the purchaser bought a townhouse in a good location. The area was perceived as one that attracted young professionals as well as blue-collar workers interested in medium-priced housing with good area schools and services. In this case, the drawback was not based on any failings in the area or the location or the perceptions related to that area, but in the economics of the situation.

In this particular case, the townhouse was a resale. The original owner had purchased at preconstruction prices several years before our client. When he sold it, he took a substantial profit. The townhouse was then purchased at its current market value, which already included the initial appreciation. The value was still rising, but at a slower pace. In addition, most purchasers in that area were, like my client, first-time homeowners. They purchased in that area because it was less expensive yet offered great family-style services. New purchasers were in the same situation my client was in when he started out and could not afford to pay huge housing costs. Therefore, the price of the houses, and the growth potential of the investment, was limited by the purchasing power of potential buyers. Once again, our client did make a profit on his sale, but his reliance solely on the location of the property, near good schools, represented a less than ideal choice in terms of his investment.

CONSIDER ALL THREE FACTORS: AREA, PERCEPTION, AND ECONOMICS

The key to making the best investment in real estate, and specifically in condos, co-ops, and townhouses, is to consider all three factors: area, perception, and economics. Investing in real estate represents a certain dedication on the part of the purchaser. Given the axiom that any purchase of real estate is an investment, your investment should be purchased with an eye toward maximum economic rewards, even when your primary interest is in buying your home for personal use. We have posited that an investment in real estate made solely upon the location of the property will not yield those results. Rather, it is necessary to incorporate three considerations prior to making an investment:

1. *Consider the overall area.* This incorporates location factors, but that alone is not enough.

2. *Consider perceptions others have of the area.* Do the local residents consider it strictly a commercial or tourist area with no history of residential development? Are you going to be a pioneer investor? Do you want to be? Sometimes, the greater the risk, the greater the reward, but that is not always true, especially in real estate.

3. *Consider the economic factors.* How big a down payment can you afford, and can you carry the property on a month-to-month basis? Are there less-expensive apartments that meet your personal needs? If they do, are they as good an investment in the long term? What are real or projected carrying costs, real estate taxes?

In the following chapters, we are going to look at all of these questions as they relate to the purchase and sale of condominiums, co-ops, townhouses, and hotel-condos and timeshares as appropriate, so that your investment will be an optimal one from both a personal and financial standpoint.

CHAPTER 3

In the previous chapter, we discussed some of the things you can do prior to beginning your search for a real estate investment. By now you should have some concept of what type of property you are looking for and how much you can afford. Perhaps you visited a bank and received a prequalification letter from your lending institution. Now you are ready to search in earnest and have selected an area that you feel suits your needs.

You have decided that you wish to purchase a condominium apartment. You know you will need a building that is pet friendly, has indoor parking, and has a gymnasium. You plan to use the property as a primary residence but may wish to rent it if you get promoted at your job, which would mean a transfer to another city for at least two years. Because time is a precious commodity, you elect to visit a local broker who has come highly recommended by your friends as being professional and knowledgeable in the area you are interested in.

THE PROCESS BEGINS

Upon your visit to the broker, the first thing you should do is indicate what type of property you are interested in and what price range you are looking for. Be as specific as possible with regard to details, especially regarding these seven factors:

1. Consider the type of property you are interested in purchasing: a condo, co-op, townhouse, hotel-condominium, or timeshare. (As this is a personal residence, the last two will not be a consideration in most cases.) You may be undecided. If so, check all the available types to help you compare and contrast. Tables 3-1 and 3-2 may be helpful in organizing your thoughts.

2. Identify how many bedrooms and bathrooms you want.

3. Find out whether the building allows pets, specifically your pet. Dogs and cats are the main types of pets, although some owners have more exotic animals. Let the broker know up front what pet you have and, if it is a dog, how much it weighs. Some buildings allow dogs but only up to a certain weight limit.

4. Tell the broker if you have a preference for a certain specific location within the area of interest. However, be open to suggestions. Being rigid is not a good thing when searching for property because you may miss a good opportunity. For example, a building may offer only one assigned parking space but have valet service for the second car. If the unit represents a good purchase, don't close your mind to this selection simply on the basis of a parking space. Also, if the price for what you want is prohibitive, are you willing to look at other areas, or do you want to stick with the area of choice but try for a smaller unit, perhaps a one bedroom instead of two?

Table 3-1. Comparison Worksheet.

Property	Cooperative A	Condo B	Townhouse C
Type of Investment	Corporate shares— unit assigned	Real estate— deed in fee simple	Real estate— deed in fee simple
Price	$650,000	$800,000	$450,000
Monthly Fee	$500.00	$650.00	$300.00
Annual Taxes	$13,000	$16,000	$9,000
Square Footage (living area not including terraces or balconies)	1,200	1,100	1,300
Price per Square Foot	$500	$666.66	$409.09

Table 3-2. Additional Worksheet.

Property	Cooperative A	Condo B	Townhouse C	Winner
Floor Plan	3	4	5	C
elevators, community rooms	2	4	1	B
Estimated Appreciation★	3	5	2	B
Personal Preference	4	5	3	B

★You can calculate this by looking at the "solds" for the comparables to your unit and the tax rolls to see what the sellers originally paid. This information is contained in the public records, and your Realtor can supply them to you from the MLS.

5. Determine what kind of amenities you require. For example, you might insist that the building have a gymnasium and indoor parking for two cars, one for you and one for your spouse.

6. Tell the broker what appliances you require in the unit. Most units have these standard appliances: an oven, a refrigerator, and a cooktop.

   What about some others appliances? How about a microwave, dishwasher, or washer/dryer? Many owners want their units to have a washer and dryer in the apartment as opposed to sharing a common-element laundry room. Older buildings may not allow it. This leads us to the next consideration.

7. Decide whether you have a preference for an older building or new construction. Older buildings may be more attractive architecturally or offer a better deal than new construction. However, if the building is really old, it may be subject to state or federal Historic Preservation Act legislation. This usually means that the facade of the building may not be altered without going through a

lengthy process that is both expensive and time consuming and may result in denial of a needed project. This could mean problems with necessary upgrading or renovation of the building. Also, as indicated in point #6, new construction may offer more amenities and appliances. What about floors and views? Do you want a high floor or low, and what type of view are you interested in?

LOOKING AT PROPERTIES

At this point, the broker should have enough information to begin his or her search. Brokers, especially those designated as Realtors, have a variety of tools available to help you in the search. Most Realtors have brochures from all the major developments in the area and are prepared to go with you to new projects. A good Realtor will know the developers with the best reputations for building good and successful projects. Also, the Realtor will have access to the Multiple Listing Service (MLS), or Exchange (MLX), as it is now known in some areas. The Realtor should be able to produce a list of suitable properties to show you.

A smart broker will not show you too many units at one time. Aside from the fact that it is tiring, viewing too many properties at one showing tends to confuse buyers. We generally recommend that you see no more than four apartments per session. Many buyers bring a notebook to make notes on each unit. This is not necessary. Your broker should be able to give you a fact sheet on each unit he or she shows you.

INSPECTING THE BUILDING

Be sure to take a tour of the building. Here are some items to note during the tour:

1. Is the building well kept? Does the outside of the building seem faded? Does it look like it will soon need a paint job? Painting buildings is expensive and may mean a special assessment will be forthcoming. Is the lobby clean, the staff (if any) friendly and courteous? If there is valet parking, does the valet attend you upon your arrival? Does he or she open your door and welcome you?

2. Is the building located in an area you find acceptable? Is the building located close to work, shopping, entertainment, religious services, banking, medical services, public transportation. Do you feel

that the surrounding environment is safe? Do you feel confident walking in the area at night?

3. Is the elevator to the unit clean? Does it make weird noises? Do

metal or wood? Does it look solid?

8. As you enter the unit, what is the view from the window (if any)? When you walk in, is the first thing you see another building, a park, an ocean?

9. Is the building naturally light, or dim? Try to note your initial reaction because that will probably be the same reaction of anyone you may want to rent or sell the unit to in the future.

10. Do the hallways smell? If so, what are those smells—dampness, cooking odors?

11. Is the hallway noisy? Do you hear people talking inside of their units? Do you hear loud music or televisions while you are walking down the hallway to your apartment?

It is now time to take a tour of the unit itself. In some cases, the unit may be the broker's own listing, in which case he or she will personally show you the unit, or the unit may be the listing of another or cooperating broker. If there is a cooperating broker involved, that person will generally conduct the tour.

Here are some points to keep in mind while the tour is being conducted:

Kitchen

1. Are the appliances in good repair?

2. Is there any warranty on the appliances? Some owners purchase appliance insurance after the initial factory warranty expires. These policies are transferable to the new owners and are prorated at the

closing. We'll explain prorations later in the book. For now, if you bought the unit, you would get credit for the unused portion of the warranty.

3. Does the unit have the appliances you want?

4. Is it an eat-in kitchen?

5. Does the kitchen meet your needs? Would you enjoy preparing meals there? If you don't think you would, probably neither would anyone else you might care to sell or rent it to in the future. Always remember that real estate is an investment, even if you are going to initially use it yourself. In this case, you may want to rent or sell it if you get that promotion.

6. Is the kitchen well lit and well ventilated?

7. Are the cooking (cook-top) appliances gas or electric?

Living Room/Dining Room Area

1. Is there a separate (formal) dining area?

2. Is the living room sufficient?

3. Is it cable ready?

4. Is there a convenient phone jack? (Even wireless phones require at least one phone jack somewhere in the apartment.)

5. If you are bringing furniture, will if fit? (This question applies to each room.)

Bedrooms

For our example, you have requested a two-bedroom, two-bath unit.

1. Are the two bedrooms side by side, or is it a split bedroom plan (bedrooms separated by the living room)?

2. Will they hold your furniture?

3. Are the phone jacks and cable plugs in places that will accommodate your furniture layout?

4. Is there sufficient closet space for your wardrobe? Do the closets have shelving?

5. Do you like the views, especially in the master bedroom?

Bathrooms

1. Does the master bath (the one you'll be using) have a shower or tub? Do you have a preference? Is there a bidet? (If you don't know what it is, you don't need it.) There should be...

5. Is the guest bath adequate? You should use the same guidelines for evaluating the guest bathroom.
6. Do the bathrooms have sufficient towel racks (heated perhaps)?

General Observations

1. Flooring
   a. Is there carpeting, tile, wood, or marble? What is the quality?
   b. What kind of condition is it in?
2. Window Treatments
   a. Are there curtains or shades?
   b. If you are buying in a tropical climate, are there black-out curtains to protect and shield from the sun? What about hurricane shutters or windows that can resist wind and rain?
3. Walls and Ceilings
   a. Do the walls and ceilings have cracks or damp spots (brownish tint)? This may be an indication of structural or water damage to the unit.
   b. Do you hear anyone in the next apartment or in the hallway? What about street noise? What do you hear? Do you smell any cooking from other units? This is a time to allow your senses to do some work. Smell and hearing tell a lot about a unit. When possible, I try to gain entrance to the adjoining apartment while my wife remains in the unit. I yell and scream some message to my wife to ascertain if she can hear it.
4. Air Conditioning and Heating
   a. Is it central or individual units?

b. Are they warrantied?

c. What type of heating and air conditioning does the apartment have? Have they been tested lately? If the air conditioning units are individual, how old are they?

SCARY STUFF YOU SHOULD ASK ABOUT

Mold

Mold is a serious problem. If you have mold, it can be a danger to your health, and it is costly to remove, if it even can be removed. It is generally caused by moisture in the unit. Mold is not only found in old buildings but can be found in new construction as well. We have heard of new buildings that, due to construction delays complicated by adverse weather conditions, acquired mold problems in the units during construction. In some states, the problem is so severe that mold disclosures are a required part of the contract. Mold is not always readily detectible by smell or sight. It can be found in the air ducts of the apartment. Air-quality samples can be taken to detect mold if you inspect the unit as part of your contract rights. We will discuss inspections in the chapter on contracts, Chapter 7.

Asbestos

Some older buildings constructed in the 1950s and early 1960s were built with asbestos in the walls to retard fire. The problem with asbestos is that in friable form—that is, when it is in the air, it can cause cancer if you inhale it. Imagine you are hammering a nail for a picture into the wall and some asbestos dust gets in your lungs. In the unlikely event that you were to get cancer from asbestos, it would take about 20 years to develop, so it is tough to pinpoint. Nevertheless, I know of a few apartments that do have asbestos in the walls. As long as you don't disturb the wall, it is safe; but once disturbed, it is best to avoid it. If you are looking at apartments that were built prior to the 1970s, I would ask if the walls contain asbestos, just to be sure.

Lead-Based Paint

Today's paints do not contain lead. However, older units may have been painted with lead-based paint, which is dangerous if ingested (generally by children who might swallow paint chips). Various state laws require that sellers disclose if the paint on their walls contains lead. These are usually in buildings constructed prior to 1978. Generally, the cure for lead-based paint problems is to scrape the walls and repaint with new, nonleaded paint.

Fire Alarms and Exits

Children

Most state laws will govern how an association may treat children. Obviously, if you have children, this is going to be a key factor. Generally, it is illegal not to allow children in a building unless that building is legally designated as being strictly for senior citizens. Your broker will know the laws regarding children. Some useful questions regarding children should include the following:

1. Are there amenities for children, such as a playroom?
2. Are the rules of the building kid friendly?
3. Are there other families with children living in the building? If so, about how many?
4. Is there school bus pick-up at or near the building?
5. How are the local area schools rated?
6. How close are the schools to the building?

Guests

Some buildings have rules concerning guests. You might wish to ask the following questions:

1. How many guests can you have in the unit for extended (more than a few days) visits?
2. If you are unmarried according to state law, does a live-in companion or significant other or domestic partner as the case may be, need to be approved by the board of directors?

3. Are there any other rules which apply to guests that you should be aware of?

Amenities

Let us suppose that for argument's sake, you love this unit. Is that it? Of course not; you still need to ask more questions. First, recall that a gymnasium was a priority for you. Without indicating your reaction to the unit, tell the broker you now wish to see the amenities—in this case, the gymnasium.

Amenities are important. They add value to the building and, specifically, to your unit. The more amenities, the more value added to the building. The downside is that these amenities cost money to maintain, and that adds costs to your monthly charges. However, if you can afford it, go with the most amenities. It is worth it, both for personal quality of life and rental and resale value.

You have indicated that you are concerned about having a gymnasium. The building has a rooftop swimming pool and a gymnasium as amenities. It also has a sauna and locker rooms. Here some questions to reflect upon while touring the facilities:

Gymnasium

1. Is the gym equipment new?
2. Is it well cared for?
3. Is there an attendant?
4. Are towels provided?
5. Is there sufficient equipment for your needs?
6. What are the hours of operation?

Pool

1. Is it clean?
2. Is the water blue (indicating it is well kept and properly chlorinated)?
3. Does it meet your needs?
4. Is it attended?
5. What are the operating hours?

Sauna and Locker Rooms

1. Are they clean?
2. Is the sauna operational?

charges and are viewed as a negative factor.

Again, for argument's sake, let us suppose the amenities are excellent. What do you do now?

BUYER'S TIP: I recommend that you return to the unit for another visit. Walk around, soak in the atmosphere. Try to picture yourself living there. Does it feel right?

I recall attempting to sell a property to a prospective buyer. The unit met the buyer's every request, and I was able (in true salesperson form) to overcome every objection. But the buyer kept saying, "I know it's what I asked for, but it just doesn't feel right. The vibes are wrong." I didn't make the sale, but I understand what the buyer was saying. Buying a property is an emotional event, no matter how much we try to make it scientific. So go with the flow and listen to those vibes. Unfortunately, once your *zen* experience is over, we have to return to the earthly world of contracts and money and some more questions you should be asking.

Let's assume you like the unit. What do you do next? The first thing to do is resist the temptation to make an offer right away. Brokers are salespeople and will try to create a sense of urgency. But unless you are absolutely sure you must have this unit, see what else is out there. Take the brochure or sales sheet on the unit and note your thoughts on it. Then proceed with the tour.

BROCHURES AND INFORMATION: WHAT SHOULD YOU ASK FOR?

If you like a unit, ask for as much information about it as you can. You may not be able to get it all, but if you don't ask, the answer will always be no, so you have nothing to lose by trying. Here is a list of five things you may wish to obtain:

1. Floor plans
2. Rules and regulations of the building
3. Condo or cooperative documents
4. Application forms
5. Copy of the budget

You may be able to get floor plans if the owner has them or if there are some in the management office. You may be able to get a copy of the rules and regulations if they are separate from the association documents. You probably won't be able to get a copy of the association documents until you make an offer in writing. Condo and co-op documents are expensive, and if the owner doesn't get them back, there is usually a charge for obtaining a new copy. Many states require that you receive these documents in order for the contract to be enforceable, so don't worry, eventually you will get a set. In Chapter 7 on paperwork, we will go into more detail on how to read and understand them.

YOU'VE NARROWED YOUR SELECTION: HOW DO YOU CHOOSE?

Let's assume that you have conducted your tours, studied your floor plans, checked the areas, and done your economics. You have narrowed your selection to two apartments in two different buildings. What's next?

You should call the broker and arrange to see both apartments again. Some people prefer to take another party with them—a parent, relative, or friend—to help them decide. We prefer to go alone. After all, it is your purchase, and you need to make the decision. You have done the research, and you should make the final decision.

Here are some questions you may wish to ask and information you should seek in conjunction with your final decision:

1. Why is the owner selling? People, (myself included) feel obliged to ask this question as if it had great probative value. I can assure you in 25 years in real estate, nobody has ever said in response to this question, "Gosh, I'm selling because the upstairs neighbor

gives flamenco lessons at 2 A.M., the building is poorly run, the board of directors raises the maintenance each year and it has become unaffordable, and there are strange odors when the wind shifts." The standard answers are "We ~~~ ~~ ~ ~

~~ ~~~~~~~~, get a list of comparable apartments in the building that have sold in the last six months to a year. This list should include the price they were listed for and the final price they sold for and how long they were on the market prior to closing. This is public information and is available online from records in the county court and it is a feature of the Multiple Listing Service (MLS), which your broker can get in about five seconds.

3. You should know the monthly maintenance charges and annual taxes for the apartments you are considering. This will be given to you by the broker as well.

4. When you are in the building, try to talk to the residents. Tell them you are considering buying an apartment in the building and watch their reactions. If they are truly happy, they will wax prolific on how they love the building. If they are not, I assure you they will vent. Listen to what their complaints are. Based on your observations, do you think they are valid? If you are not sure, investigate further. Talk to the manager if you need to verify information you received from a resident.

5. You can ask what kind of people live in the building, as long as you restrict your question to general attributes such as married couples, retirees, young executives, and other general categories of that nature. You cannot and should not ask questions concerning race, creed, color or national origin. Realtors are prohibited by law from answering questions of that nature, and it is improper to ask them.

6. You should also ask if there are any upcoming special assessments or fees. The seller is required to tell you of any *announced or declared*

special assessments, but it is a gray area as to whether or not the seller has to disclose special assessments that are being considered but not *officially* placed on an agenda to be discussed by the board of directors. Morally, everything should be disclosed, but what a seller must legally do is another matter. Most sellers don't disclose special assessments that haven't been placed on an agenda, and so it up to you to ask the question. Most sellers, if they know a special assessment is coming, will tell the truth and disclose if you ask them point blank. How special assessments are handled is based on your contract. We will discuss this in Chapter 7 on paperwork.

7. You might try to find out what your seller originally paid for the property. This issue is placed last because it is not as important as most buyers think, although every buyer wants to know how much profit the seller is making (ourselves included). However, it is the market that controls the price of the property, not the seller nor the buyer. How much the seller makes on his investment is a function of the laws of supply and demand, not the buyer's limitations on how much profit he or she is going to allow the seller to make. What this type of information may tell you is the overall rate of appreciation. We will discuss this further at the end of this chapter and in Chapter 10 on selling your unit. Your broker's MLS contains this information from the county tax rolls. We will discuss the specifics of making the offer in the following chapters.

You Made the Choice: Any More Questions?

The answer is yes, you probably have a great many more questions, but there is some good news. Most states require that the seller disclose in writing any information that may "materially" affect your purchase of his or her property. Each state has its own procedures, but generally, once you sign a contract and the seller accepts your price and terms, in order for the contract to be enforceable against you, you must receive documents that disclose and answer the following questions:

1. Do you need the approval of the board of directors before you can buy the unit?

2. What kind of approval do you need to do renovations and improvements?

3. Are there any special assessments upcoming?

4. Is the building currently involved in any lawsuits?

5. How soon after you purchase can you lease the unit and what is

 your rights as an owner (i.e., voting procedures)?

If you have not already obtained a copy of the rules and regulations, they will be part of the association documents. In the chapter on paperwork, Chapter 7, we will further discuss how to read the association documents and what information to look for in them.

IMPORTANT POINT: Remember that each state differs on procedure. Be sure to understand what your state's procedure is prior to signing a contract.

For example, are there rescission periods that allow you to withdraw your offer if you don't like what your read in the condominium documents? If not, then you should demand to see these documents before you sign any contract. In Florida, with the purchase of a condominium, after you sign a contract, the seller must give you a seller's disclosure form containing the information discussed previously, the condominium documents, and the association's budget. If you are buying from a developer, you have 15 business days to review these documents and withdraw your offer or if you purchase a resale, 3 business days to review the documents.

These rules may vary with townhouse, timeshare, and cooperative purchases, which are governed by different sections of the law. Hotel-condos are generally treated the same as condominiums for rescission purposes.

Your realtor or attorney will advise you on these laws, and you should know them *before you sign a contract.*

SUPER IMPORTANT POINT: Although we will discuss in some detail how to read and interpret association documents, this is no substitute for consulting with a qualified attorney.

Such issues as what happens to the property if you should die depend in part on whether you are dealing with real estate (condominiums and townhouses) or cooperatives (corporate shares). The time to discuss these matters with your lawyer is *before* your contract becomes final and enforceable under your state's laws.

Other topics you may wish to discuss are, whose name should the deed be in, and what happens in case of divorce or separation? We will discuss these issues, but in general terms only. You should know and understand specifically your state's laws and how they apply to your own personal situation.

USING COMPARATIVE TABLES

If you are unsure of what type of property you want to buy, it might be helpful to review the worksheet in Table 3-1.

Some buyers may wish to include the information in Table 3-2 in their decision-making process. Simply assign a value to each category—for example, 1 to 5, 1 being the lowest and 5 being the highest—and see how each property stacks up.

As you can see, the winner is B, the condominium. Although charts like these are not by any means scientific nor guarantee that you will make the best selection, they are useful in organizing your thoughts. You can use these models to add other categories such as financing. In the next chapters, we will discuss more specifically the technical aspects of the actual purchase.

CHAPTER 4

In this chapter we begin our process of purchasing a property. We will first discuss buying directly from the developer of a project, and then in the following chapter discuss the purchase of a resale.

As we proceed, we will explore the process and ramifications of purchasing directly from a developer. We will discuss the advantages and disadvantages to you, the purchaser, and what you should expect when you visit a developer's sales office. We will tell you what questions to ask before making an offer and how to most effectively negotiate a transaction with the developer's representative. First, let's take a quick look at the advantages and disadvantages of buying directly from a developer.

ADVANTAGES OF BUYING FROM A DEVELOPER

1. *Your unit will be new.* The most obvious reason for buying directly from a developer is the fact that you will be buying something new—something never used by anyone else. Let's face it—what would you prefer, new clothes or used clothes? New appliances or used appliances? New is very appealing. Almost everything from the roof to the refrigerator comes with some type of warranty. New also intimates the latest technology, the best of everything.

57

2. ***The price might be lower.*** Buying directly from the developer also suggests a better price, the developer's price. The idea is that you get in on the ground floor (no pun intended) because as units in the building become more scarce, the prices will rise.

3. ***The selection is better.*** Depending on how early in the development process you are buying, buying from a developer gives you the opportunity to select a more favorable unit in terms of size, floor level and position, exposure (views), and so on.

4. ***Improvement is possible to the basic unit.*** Sometimes, but not always, if it is early enough in the process, you may be able to contract for upgrades to the unit that the developer might not be willing to give later on. Also, you may have wider selection of colors and types of upgrades such as tile, carpet or marble, color of paint, and appliances.

5. ***You can anticipate appreciation.*** Because real estate tends to appreciate over time rather than depreciate in value, the price of a condo purchased new from a developer is likely to rise—in some cases, rise quite rapidly. As a result, you may have more flexibility and may be able to maximize your profit if and when you decide to sell. One outgrowth of the rapid appreciation of new property is that some people will choose to sell their units before they ever occupy them. This concept is often referred to as *flipping*. We will discuss flipping later in this chapter.

Disadvantages of Buying from a Developer

1. ***You might pay more.*** Although it is true that you can save money by buying new, it is also possible that new construction will be more expensive than an existing project due to increased building costs, possible increased costs of materials and labor, as well as higher costs of acquiring the raw land to construct. It may also be more expensive for you to get financing for a new project as opposed to one already in existence. This is where you are going to have to rely on your research to evaluate costs and your personal feelings on what you prefer, or which you believe to be an overall better investment.

2. ***There are hidden costs.*** With new construction, many costs can only be estimated. For example, the exact taxes for your unit have not yet been assessed, and developers tend to underestimate the maintenance costs to make the purchase more attractive. We usually expect at least a 15 percent increase in the monthly maintenance assessment when the new board of directors takes over from the developer. Sometimes it can be more.

3. *The project may stall.* Buying into a development that is not yet completed (preconstruction) is never a sure thing. There are usually construction delays or acts of God such as weather-related problems or labor problems. There could also be delays in getting supplies such .... ̕

...., of course, affect the value of the property, making it difficult if not impossible to resell. You should check your contract to find out what protections are offered to you in this regard. If the contract doesn't specify it, ask the developer's representative. Be sure to find out who the escrow agent is for the project. That should be the company you make your deposit check to. Most reputable developers will use only a part of the deposit toward construction, and part will remain in escrow. You should also check your state's laws regarding developer's use of deposit money.

4. *New buildings often have unforeseen problems.* These might be minor and easily fixed, but others can require major structural repairs. Although many states have laws that allow the owners to sue the developers and their insurance companies for construction defects, litigation is costly and time consuming, both in terms of hiring competent attorneys as well as engineers to provide the necessary studies to prove your case.

New boards of directors are encouraged to hire engineers and conduct an engineering study prior to the expiration of the time allowed (statute of limitations) to complain to a developer and file suit if necessary. This will generally result in a special assessment against the unit owners.

GOING THROUGH THE PROCESS OF BUYING FROM A DEVELOPER

You have made the decision to purchase from a developer. You are secure in your calculations as to what you can spend on the purchase. For example, you have $50,000 in cash and you qualify for financing up to $200,000.

KEEP IN MIND: If you have $50,000 in cash and qualify for $200,000 in financing, remember that there are going to be closing costs and possibly you will incur other costs such as furnishing the unit, perhaps the hiring of a moving company, and other expenses related to acquiring your new home. Be careful to factor these expenses in.

If you are familiar with the area you are buying in, a good portion of your research is already done. You know about the transportation, school systems, recreational areas, and other aspects of the surrounding community. If you are relocating to a new area, you may wish to engage a local broker. As we have already indicated, a broker can be quite helpful, so even if you are staying in your own area, you may certainly wish to hire a broker.

Brokers should be familiar with the new developments in the area beyond having a brochure and some general information. A qualified professional will know about the developers and their construction history, what stages the different developments are at, which developments are selling well (fast), and which are attracting speculators as opposed to those purchasers who are actually planning to occupy their units. A broker may represent several new properties under development, including townhouses, condominiums, and cooperatives. Once on site, some brokers may not participate in the sales process and leave the selling portion to the developer's sales staff. However, a good broker will participate and ask relevant questions on behalf of you, his or her client, as appropriate.

Visiting the Sales Office on Your Own

Let's say you decide to first visit some new developments without a broker. As you begin your exploration of new projects, you will find that most developer's representatives have a standard type of presentation and fit into a basic pattern. Within that pattern, there are some salespeople who are more aggressive, while others are content to present the project and try to work with you to help you get what you are looking for. As long as you stay focused on what you want and avoid being pressured into making an immediate decision, you'll be okay.

The First Impression: Fantasy and Flash

You (and your spouse, friend or significant other) are driving around the area in which you are planning to buy. You see a sign for a building that looks like something out of a science fiction movie. It is all glass with massive terraces. Simply stunning. About 50 feet ahead is an entrance to a construction site where the advertised building is to be built.

You remember seeing a picture of the building in the newspaper, but that picture gave the impression that the building was already completed. You now realize that it must have been computer generated. The building in the picture must have been digitally inserted into the lot, and

g the interior of the lobby is very futuristic with bright silvers and deep blues. In the lobby's center, there is a giant replica of the tower, complete with tennis courts, swimming pools, and a giant three-dimensional mockup of the beach and ocean, with miniature figurines cavorting about. In the background, there is soft music playing. You can't quite place the melody but it is somehow soothing, like elevator music, only less tacky. Your initial reaction is, "Let's get out of here; this is way out of our league." But your spouse responds, "Let's check it out. The ad in the paper said, starting prices at $275,000, which is only a little out of our range, and besides, it'll be fun to see."

BUYER'S TIP: Don't be impressed by the glitter and flash. It has been set up to be impressive, specifically to impress you, the potential buyer or *prospect*. Stay focused on the fact that you are doing objective research on purchasing a home and a real estate investment.

Meeting and Greeting and Taking the Tour

A handsome young man dressed in black approaches and introduces himself as Raul and offers you soft drinks, wine, or champagne while you wait. You are advised that a salesperson will be with you shortly, but in the meantime he, Raul, will show you the model. Raul is also quick to point out that he is not a licensed real estate agent and cannot answer any specific questions about the property.

As you and your spouse or companion walk toward the model, you find yourself surrounded by pictures of people—presumably, future residents—being pampered by waiters in formal attire serving champagne, valets in light opera military uniforms (complete with pill box hats), and a masseuse with a physique that would bring tears to Arnold Schwarzenegger, getting ready to massage a young lady clothed only in towels appropriately placed on her well-tanned physique. There are also pictures of apartment floor plans and pictures of the lobby and other amenities.

Your spouse recognizes that the pictures of the surrounding areas of the building do not match the reality of what was outside of the sales pavilion but you figure that this is artistic license.

Key Point: As you tour the model, note the features in the unit. Look for any indication, such as a small placard discreetly placed nearby indicating that this is not a standard feature, but rather an upgrade, *available at an additional cost*. The unit may be fabulously decorated, but it may cost you a considerable amount of money to match its features. You should ask your salesperson, not the tour guide, since presumably, the guide is prohibited from answering any specific questions, exactly what the unit comes with, included and without additional cost.

Enter the Salesperson

At the close of the tour, you'll be introduced to the salesperson. He or she may give you a quick briefing on the development's overall setup. If there is a building replica, as mentioned previously, or a detailed map, the salesperson will indicate the locations of the various units and their descriptions, the parking areas, and locations of the various amenities.

At the end of the demonstration, the salesperson may ask you to follow him or her into a conference room or office. In most cases, the salesperson will then leave you and your companion alone in the office for a short period of time. The intention is to have you start to discuss what you have seen, free of any sales pressure. The intent of the presentation thus far was to impress you with the development. If successful, the desired result is that you will actually begin "selling" yourselves on the project, picturing yourselves living there, discussing how good, how much fun your life will be at this new and exciting place.

Teaching Point: This is actually a good time to catch your breath. Instead of engaging in fantasies, discuss what you have seen from the point of view of positives and negatives. Try to cancel out the glitz and be objective. Were the rooms small, was there enough closet space, was the kitchen adequate? How about the bathrooms? Did you like them? Get past the decorations and try to envision the unit raw, without the fancy furniture and decorations. How do you feel about it now?

The Sales Pitch

The Sales Scenario

At this stage, the salesperson will often place a computerized spreadsheet on the table in front of you. It will have numbers across the top row and another set of numbers on the left side going down the page. The rest of the document has prices increasing from top to bottom in each column. The salesperson will explain that the outer left column designates the floor numbers of the building and the top row represents the unit numbers. You'll be told that the lobby, health club facilities, meeting rooms, and parking garage will take up the first six floors of the tower, and residences begin on floor seven. The remaining spaces in the rows and columns represent the prices of each unit. For example, the salesperson will demonstrate, unit #703 corresponds to $275,000. This is the least expensive unit in the building. The salesperson explains that the 03 line indicates that they are one-bedroom, one-bath units facing the west, toward the city, as was pointed out at the display.

The Creation of Urgency

Most of the prices on the sheet have been blocked out and there are very few units with prices visible. When you ask why, the salesperson will explain that the prices are blocked out because the building is 80 percent sold, even though officially, marketing to the public had only begun a few weeks ago—such was the demand for this project. The salesperson will almost certainly also point out that prices will be going up in the next week or two for the remaining units.

CAUTION: This is known as the *creation of urgency*. If you don't buy now, your opportunity to get a unit, let alone a good price, will be lost. Resist this type of pressure. Although the prices may eventually go up, they won't go up in the next day or two, and you can always offer at the original price, even if they do. Some of the classic urgency lines are as follows:

1. "We have a buyer who couldn't raise the down payment so we had to take back the unit. It's a great deal and won't last, and the prices will be going up next week."

2. "You can always rent the unit. It's a great investment, even if you can't move in right away."

3. "The appreciation on these units will be tremendous. You can flip it before closing if you change your mind and still make money."

4. (Depending on state law) "You have 15 days to make a decision; leave us a deposit and signed contract. You can always back out if you change your mind."

Reviewing the Typical Sales Experience

You have now reached the moment of truth in the sales process. The whole scenario is geared to get you to commit. What should you do? Let's go over what has happened during this sales experience and analyze it further.

First, with minor deviations to account for regional location and type of construction, the above is the basic sales technique of mid- to high-priced condominiums, townhomes, hotel-condominiums, and, if you can find one, new construction cooperatives. Developers spend a great deal of money on sales pavilions and salespeople because the tactic works. The sharp reader will wonder why a project that is 80 percent sold would require the developer to invest in a sales pavilion and staff. We will get to that point shortly, but the point is well taken. This is the kind of analysis an astute purchaser should be going through.

The other point to remember is that marketing is highly scientific. The developer ascertains what its client base will be, and the presentation is based around this determination. Developers are in the business of building projects and selling them to the target market.

Further, good salespeople know there are few *be backs*. An experienced salesperson understands that he or she will have one chance to make or *close* the deal. Once the prospective buyer walks away, the odds that he or she will return diminish greatly. There is just too much competition for the purchasing dollars, not only in the real estate market, but cars, clothes, vacations, and so on. You may walk out of the sales pavilion intending to come back and make a purchase but decide to buy a car or go on vacation instead. Or you may see another project and make that purchase instead. Thus, the salesperson will always make his or her best effort to get a deposit

their sales center, so they are going to take their best shot at closing a deal. That's fine, but you are under no obligation to make that deal on the first visit, nor should you. You can accept a soft drink or coffee, but under no circumstances accept wine or other alcoholic beverages if they are offered. Because of today's strict liability laws regarding drinking and driving, most developers won't offer you liquor, but just the same, be aware.

The Focused Client

We have a client who is always smiling and joking until it comes to viewing the property. All of a sudden, he is all business. His expression changes, he becomes serious and focused only on the transaction. That is the posture you should take. Forget about the nice pavilion, the attractive salespeople, the food, and drink. When you view the model, forget about the extra frills. Concentrate on the unit's layout and what the developer gives you with the purchase:

- Does the unit come with flooring? If so, what kind?
- Do you get a credit if you don't take the developer's flooring? If so, how much?
- What about the appliances and cabinetry?
- Are walls painted for you?
- What about the ceiling? Is it painted as well? Some aren't, which can cause cracking when the building settles.
- When will the project be completed?
- Which bank does the developer use for its financing?
- What other residential projects has this developer completed in this area?

- What amenities are included?
- How many parking spaces come with the unit? Are they assigned or deeded?

If the guide won't answer those questions, get the salesperson to take you back and ask him or her all your questions. In most cases, the list of items provided by the developer will be in the sales brochure, but it is always best to eyeball what you are and are not getting, so it is clearer in your mind when you review the documentation.

Resist, Resist, Resist—At Least on the First Visit

When you were ushered into the conference room, you were left alone for a few minutes to take in the tour and sales talk. This conference room is often called the *closing room* because this is where the salesperson will make his or her best attempt to make the sale or *close* the deal. To do this, the salesperson must create a sense of urgency. In other words, you must believe that if you don't make a deal today, you will lose your chance. Sometimes it is true and if you don't reserve a unit, you may lose a good deal. In most cases, it is not true and you can and should walk out and think about the purchase.

Rescission Periods

Because the pressure that is put to bear on a prospect to make a deal is so great, states such as Florida have a *rescission* or "cooling off" *period* where you, the purchaser, can extricate yourself from a real estate transaction for a limited period of time. This also gives you a chance to carefully review the documentation including the contract and the condominium documents (which will be discussed in Chapter 7 on paperwork). This is not true in every state, and it should always be made clear by the salesperson, what, if any, your rescission rights are.

PROFESSIONAL TEACHING POINT: The experienced real estate purchaser may wish to put down a deposit to reserve a unit while he or she studies the condominium documents, knowing he or she can get their deposit refunded. However, novice or first-time buyers should understand that although their deposit will be returned, it takes time and can be nerve racking until the money is back in the purchaser's hands. You also must be careful to follow the legal procedures in order to get your money back. Usually, this involves some sort of letter indicating that you wish to rescind and receive a refund of your deposit. A phone call to the salesperson probably won't do it.

READ AND HEED: Not all states have rescission periods and in those states that do, they may not apply to every type of real estate transaction. Rescission periods are usually disclosed in the contract, but you should ask before you sign. Not knowing about rescission periods could make you liable for the purchase at the time you give the deposit and sign the contract. We will discuss contracts in Chapter 7.

Percentage of Sales: We're 80 Percent Sold!

As already indicated, the urgency that the salespeople try to create is the idea that if you don't place your money on the table now, the product you desire may be gone. In our example, when the salesperson showed you the sales list, it had 80 percent of the units blocked out. Recall that the astute readers questioned why the developer would go to the expense of building an expensive sales pavilion if the project is 80 percent sold? There are a number of reasons for this.

First, in many cases, the developer will only release a portion of the available units for sale so that the developer may retain better control over prices. That 80 percent figure might reflect 80 percent of the inventory that the developer has released for sale, not 80 percent of the total amount of units for sale in the entire project.

BUYER'S TIP: This point can be cleared up by simply asking the sales agent the specific question, "On what is this percentage of sales based?" Most sales agents are licensed by their respective states and won't risk those licenses by lying, so assume the answer is true. The answer will probably be something to the effect that there is more property to be released but it will be at a higher price. That may or may not be accurate; it depends on the market at the time of release.

Based on the answer you receive, you now have two pieces of new and valuable information:

1. You know that their advertising is at best misleading. *Puffing,* which is exaggerating a fact, is acceptable, both legally and as a sales practice. Examples of puffing are calling a swimming pool "Olympic style" when it is merely average size, or calling a system "state of the art" when it is not actually the latest piece of equipment. However, while not necessarily illegal per se, I consider it a misrepresentation to advertise that a product is 80 percent sold if the entire product has not been released for sale.

2. You have now diminished the sense of urgency that the salesperson was attempting to convey.

Get the Big Picture

To resist the sense of urgency scenario that the developer wants to create, you have to do a little research on your own. As you find the answers to certain questions, you will know if this property is right for you and whether you should indeed consider making an immediate commitment.

How Many Units Are Really Left? One reason it is important to know what percentage of the building is sold is because you need to know *the real number* of units the developer has in inventory. If the developer only released a handful of units and the building is not selling well, the developer could "dump" the remaining units on the market to get out of the project, once it is completed, or declare bankruptcy and never complete it. Thus, if the developer sold 40 percent of its true entire inventory in the first week, that tells you there are, at least initially, robust sales. However, if the developer only released 40 units and sold 80 percent of that number, then the figures are misleading as to the real total percentage of sales, which are going to be much lower. The fact is, if a project is presold at a true 80 percent, there probably is no need for a fancy sales office unless there is another purpose. That purpose is what is known as *flipping.*

Flipping Units Before Closing. Flipping is the art of purchasing a condominium unit from a developer as soon as it hits the market (most often, before the developer even begins construction) and then reselling the contract to a third party prior to closing. It is a quicker turn-around of real

act as the broker for these resales to increase its profits. Thus, it gets to sell the original units, as well as the flippers' units. Sometimes, the developer will buy back a unit from a flipper, give the flipper his or her profit, and resell the unit a third time at a still greater profit.

Common Sense—But We'll Say It Anyway. Just because a unit hasn't been lived in, doesn't mean it is new. You can lose some of the advantage of buying directly from the developer—a first-time release of the property—if you have to pay a higher price for a flipped unit that is being handled by the developer. However, those who flip units generally want to do so quickly and will take less money than if they waited to close and possibly improve the property with flooring prior to reselling. Depending on the general market conditions, buying a *flip* may still be a good deal if you calculate that the market is hot and the property will still appreciate even more. As you can see, it often pays for the developer to invest in a fancy sales office for a variety of reasons. It is up to you to discover those reasons.

Is Anyone Actually Going to Live in the Building? You also want to know the percentage of purchasers who are planning to actually live in the building. You need to know this because, regardless of whether you want to live in your unit, lease it, or flip it, it is still an investment (remember our golden operating rule). As such, you need to have an accurate reading of the supply and demand not only from the standpoint of developer sales but of occupancy.

In other words, even if the developer sold a true 90 percent of the entire inventory the first weekend but only sold it to a handful of investors who plan to flip them, the developer is within its rights to advertise that 90 percent were sold the first weekend. Sounds great, and it is true, as far as it goes. So the developer sells the remaining 10 percent to individual purchasers and builds the building. Now come the purchasers who speculated that the prices would go up—the *spec purchasers*. These spec purchasers don't flip their units but rather, close on them, hoping to resell them at greater profits than they could with a quick flip prior to closing. What then can happen is the market becomes flooded with units for resale from the spec buyers. The prices are driven down while the market absorbs the units and eventually moves the prices back up. Even in a strong market, this can take several years.

RULE OF THUMB: You are looking for a high proportion of actual residents and a low proportion of spec buyers. The bulk of the resident owners provide stability in the building, while the few spec buyers provide the resale momentum, which helps the property appreciate. There is no exact desirable percentage of spec buyers to resident owners but you certainly would not want higher than 15 percent spec buyers to 85 percent residents as a rule of thumb.

The Buy-to-Lease Purchaser. An offshoot of the spec buyer is the *buy-to-lease purchaser*. It is important to know, to the greatest degree possible, how many purchasers intend to lease their units. Banks may be a valuable source of information here. Most banks will hesitate to lend money on buildings that have greater than 40 percent of the units for rent by the owners. As a rule, renters tend to take less care of the units and create more wear and tear in the buildings. Also, the resale value of a building with a reputation as being a "rental building" tends to be less. Owners have much less incentive to maintain and improve a building that is strictly an investment and in which they personally do not reside.

CONSIDER THIS CAREFULLY: If you conclude that more than approximately 40 percent of the new owners will lease the property and you are purchasing your unit for your primary residence, you might wish to consider another purchase.

If you are purchasing your unit with the intent of leasing, you may not be too concerned about this percentage. However, it is still of interest to

note from the standpoint of competition for rentals and general appreciation of the property. The less competition, the better, and you do want
maximum appreciation on your investment.

In general, real estate is a long-term investment. Short-term flipping

questions. You have been told what is included in the purchase and what
is not. Also, you need to know the estimated monthly maintenance fees
and taxes. These won't be established with certainty until the project is
finished, but the sales staff can provide you with a reasonable projection.
You won't get a copy of the condominium documents or the contract
unless you give a deposit, but at this point you don't really need them. (We
will discuss the condominium documents in Chapter 7.) For now, you
have been given a great deal of information to absorb.

Armed with this new-found knowledge, have the salesperson write
down the price of the unit you are interested in, take a brochure and
salesperson's business card (don't worry, you'll be given all of this anyway),
and leave the sales office. Go someplace quiet and consider your findings.
The closing room of the sales office is not the place to do this. If you really
love the project, you'll love it the next morning just as much. But you
need to take a break and consider the information you have been given.

Example: Megalopolis

Let's suppose that Megalopolis has really sold a true 80 percent of its inventory with at least 65 percent of the purchasers who intend to move into
the building as residents. Not ideal, but not bad, either. Is there any other
information that you need to know before making a decision? What about
the history of the developer? Is this the developer's first project? What else
has it developed? Some of this information will be in the brochure. If it's
not, make a phone call and ask the salesperson.

TEACHING POINT: The issue is whether you want to put down a
refundable deposit and hold the unit or resist the temptation and

gamble that the unit will still be available. We recommend that you wait and gamble. Resist the sales spiel and walk away.

Take a Look Around the Area

When you leave, take an objective look at the development itself. Then walk a few blocks in each direction. Note the neighborhood. What kind of buildings surround your project? Is it a residential area? Is there shopping within walking distance? Are there other high rise condominiums in the area? Make a mental note of the area. If there are other condominiums nearby, walk in. Talk to the front desk person, if there is one, and ask some general questions about the area. Get that person's perception of what it is like to live in this area. If you are buying oceanfront property, you will be paying a premium to live on the beach, so make sure there is actually a beach. Is it a large beach? We know of an oceanfront property where the surf comes almost to the building. There is virtually no beach. These are all things you need to know.

Take Another Look at Your Chosen Property

You are interested in making a purchase in Megalopolis. First ask the salesperson to please give you another tour of the model unit, as there are some points you wish to clarify. Ask for a floor plan of the unit. Pen in hand, take another look at the model, noting what is included and what are developer extras.

Let's suppose the purchaser gets an empty unit with lower-grade appliances and choice of flooring in the bathrooms only. The rest of the unit comes totally bare. The security systems, lighting, window and bathroom fixtures (including shower doors), as well as the other cool electronics that are in the model are all options but may be purchased separately or in a developer's package. It also turns out that the model unit is not exactly to scale, and the actual unit is a bit smaller.

TEACHING POINT: You will now need to calculate how much it will cost to "finish out" and furnish the unit. This is part of the economic considerations that will have to be calculated before you can make a final decision. Upon conclusion of the tour, you should take their brochures and information and prepare to leave.

WARNING: Be prepared for one last-ditch sales push. The salesperson does not want you to leave without a commitment because the odds that you will come back are very slim. Now that you have expressed some interest, efforts will be redoubled to at least get a deposit from you. The salesperson may tell you that the company can hold the unit for one day while you decide if you give them a

outside of the developer's sphere of influence.

Earlier we talked about evaluating a property based on area, perception, and economics (A.P.E.). All that we discussed in Chapter 2 applies here as well. It is incumbent upon you, the purchaser, to still do the same analysis regardless of the fact that you are buying directly from the developer. But it may take a bit of time, and you may find that you need a little help.

Talk to People

You and your spouse or companion should do a walk-about of the area—talk to some of the people on the street and in the local shops. You make another phone call to the salesperson, who reveals that the developer has done numerous condominium projects in the Miami/south Florida area and rattles off a bunch of them. You'll want to visit some of these projects and speak with some of the residents. Do they complain, or do most appear to be satisfied?

Here are some questions you should ask residents of buildings you are visiting:

1. Are you happy living in the building?
2. Did you purchase directly from the developer?
3. (If answer two is yes) Did the developer (substantially) produce what it promised in the brochures and sales presentations?
4. Was the original budget sufficient, or did you receive a large increase in monthly fees after the board of directors took over the condominium?

5. Did the board have to contract for lots of repairs to the building?

6. Would you buy another condominium from this developer?

Watch This: The answers you get should be taken with a grain of salt. But if you ask several residents and they all seem to have similar opinions, it should be a red flag to do further research. If possible, check another of the developer's projects and ask the same questions. See if there is a pattern with this developer's products.

Suppose the brochure also indicates that a local bank is financing the project. You crunch the numbers and, although it is a stretch, you will be able to manage the additional funds to make the down payment and carrying costs.

You may wish to consult several local real estate brokers to ascertain if the rental market is strong. If you are to rent the unit during the winter season, the local brokers can help with that, too.

Teaching Point: While leasing out your unit may not totally defray the carrying costs, it can significantly reduce them to a point where supporting the unit will not be a financial burden. In addition, if you lease the unit on an annual basis, the unit will carry itself and even throw off a profit.

Using a Broker

Thus far, we have considered that you elected to visit the project without a real estate broker. While it is true that there are brokers who merely tour the client to as many sites as they can and hope the sales staff of the development will make a sale, that is not indicative of all brokers. Before concluding our discussion of making a purchase from a developer, a few words about engaging a broker are mandated.

A good broker is not only an invaluable research tool, but can cut your time in finding a suitable project. Real estate brokers in the United States are generally subject to state laws. Just as there are good lawyers, good accountants, and good doctors, there are good real estate brokers who know their profession and who work and act on behalf of the client. They bring to the table, an expertise and perspective that the lay person does not generally have, although when it comes to real estate, a great many lay people think that they are experts. Unfortunately, purchasers have come to the conclusion that they can negotiate just as well themselves, and the developer will gladly pass on any savings on commissions to them. As we shall shortly see, in the vast majority of cases, this is false and exemplifying of a naive, rather than sophisticated, view of a real estate purchase.

in most (although not any) cases, the sales staff of the developer are on commission as well, so when a broker is involved in the deal, the commission is split between the sales agent of the developer and the representative broker. In no way does the purchaser reap any economic rewards from not using a broker. Quite the contrary, the good broker will know approximately, and sometimes, exactly, how much play a developer has with regard to price and will invariably negotiate a better deal for the purchaser than he or she could do themselves. In addition, the broker will provide assistance and service during the course of the transaction, such as helping with documentation and financing.

KEY POINT: A good broker knows the area developers and can gauge investment risks and returns with the client with information not available in a brochure.

PRICING ISSUES

Key to your investment in real estate is price. There are numerous issues and factors to consider. Let's take a look at some of the issues that affect pricing.

The Price Goes Up

After several days you are anxious to conclude the deal. You call the salesperson and are advised that the unit you were interested in is still available, but the developer has now raised the prices. Now you may want to call one of the real estate brokers you interviewed during your research on rental possibilities and explain the situation.

This is an example of how the participation of a broker can help a deal.

Although the developer has raised its prices, other factors besides the law of supply and demand may be operating. The broker tracks the developments and is aware of factors that make negotiating reasonable.

Since you went to the developer on your own, technically the developer is within its right to refuse to pay the broker a commission. But most reputable developers will not refuse to deal with a broker if it helps close the deal.

In your case, let's say the broker contacts the salesperson, who he knows, and sets up a meeting. He tells you the price of the unit is now $325,000, but suggests offering $275,000 and seeing what happens. He also suggests that you bring your checkbook and be ready to give at least a $10,000 down payment.

Other Factors Affecting Price

These *other factors* may involve the developers financing. Construction loans are generally incremental in nature. The developer needs to show a certain amount of sales before the bank will advance more money. This is commonly known as the *draw* on funds. In addition, even though Megalopolis has brisk sales, the particular unit you are interested in buying does not have the best view. Therefore, its main attraction is that it sells at a cheaper price. This allows less affluent people the opportunity to purchase in a luxury building.

Finally, a quick sale may look good on the developer's books based on a "bird in the hand" theory. Since most developers do not use their own funds, they also carry mortgages on each unsold unit. Each sale they make reduces their debt to the bank. Consequently, it may be in the developer's interest at this point in time to accept the offer and take less of an up-front profit but reduce its overall debt to the bank.

Let's Negotiate

You and your broker offer $275,000 and are prepared to sign a contract. If the salesperson knows that the offer will not be accepted, it will be rejected outright. (Many times the salesperson will try to deflect the blame to the bank from the developer by stating something like, "The bank won't allow the developer to accept such a low offer.") At that point, you could walk out again, but in a robust market, the developer could probably get more than the $275,000 offered and will wait. If the salesperson thinks there is a chance of acceptance, or possibly a counteroffer by the developer, he or she will take the contract and present it to the developer.

NEGOTIATING TIP:

the outcome of the transaction.

Don't Second-Guess Yourself

You have just purchased a condominium for $290,000. A few questions should arise. The first is, what advantage did you have by waiting? Should you not have bought the condominium during your first visit to the project and negotiated a better deal? You could have also made an initial offer and used the rescission period if it didn't work out.

The answer is no. Unless you absolutely know what you are doing and are an experienced real estate person, you need to do your research first. Hindsight is always 20/20. After the research is done and the deal is made, it is easy to look back and say, "Gee, I could have done it this way or that way and come out better." In this case, your research indicated that this was a good developer and its buildings were a success. What if you found a "smoking gun," such as that most of the residents of other buildings you spoke with were dissatisfied with the developer's products, and you found their reasons legitimate?

The other point to always remember when dealing with developers is that they are looking to make the maximum profit possible. They are not concerned with how many buildings they put on the market or on long-term supply and demand scenarios. As long as the market is brisk, they will build. When there is an overflow of one type of product—for example, condominiums—they will try a different approach to selling a project. Hence, the relatively new concepts of condominium-hotels, or the time shares or vacation villas or a combination of all three in one giant project. The developer's job is to build and sell while watching the bottom line. Your job is buy into a project that will appreciate over time and to give yourself the time you need to watch your bottom line. They know their target market; you should know your developer.

As you will see more clearly in Chapter 7, when you purchase from a developer, you are buying something new and presumably at a price that will give you maximum appreciation in the long term. The downside is that the developer is generally in a position of greater strength in the deal than you are, and since the project is new, you are speculating as to what the eventual outcome will be.

Teaching Point: If you do your homework and resist the pressure to make a purchase to get the best price, and do the research, you will do better in the long run.

There is a theory among some business people that the only way to buy property, new or resale, is when there is blood on the streets—in other words, when the seller is so absolutely desperate that he or she practically pays you to buy the property. For some reason, people like to brag about the fact that they did so. Although there is a specific business of buying foreclosures, which takes a certain expertise, and which is beyond the scope of this book, these plans only tend to work where the property, rather than the seller, is desperate. In other words, you can do it, but you are just going to assume someone else's burden.

A related theory of purchasing is waiting for the market to drop to make the purchase. This also doesn't work, because real estate in the long term tends to appreciate rather than depreciate, and most people will not want to give away their property. The so-called *prophets of doom* who wait for the market to drop often wind up missing the good opportunities. The irony of this type of thinking is that when there is a flux in the market and prices drop, rather than take advantage of the price, they opine that since the market is bad, this isn't the time to invest. Obviously, you can't have it both ways.

The conclusion, then, is not to try to outsmart the real estate market but join in it and make your investment. Do the research, ask the questions, run the numbers, and if it works, take the plunge.

Enjoy Yourself, Have Fun, but Be Careful

Up until now, we have tried to view real estate as strictly an investment to be made with cold calculation. But it is also fun. A large part of your research will be looking at houses and apartments. If you are thinking about a hotel-condominium, you will be looking at hotels and resorts. If you are buying directly from the developer, you will undoubtedly be treated to some first-class service while you explore beautiful ~~~

~~~ your common sense. To a great extent, they hope for the impulse buy. Their sales pavilions are not geared to the dispassionate investor. Those people buy before the sales office is even built and flip the contract before closing. What is being argued here is that you can have it both ways. Love at first sight is fine, but do the research nevertheless.

The final decision to make a purchase of real estate must be your own, and you must assume full responsibility for that purchase. There is a great temptation to lay the research or responsibility on others. We have clients who dearly want to purchase a second home but won't because their daughter keeps telling them it is a bad investment. Of course, the daughter has her own business and wants to keep her parents as financially liquid as possible. Another client was ready to make an investment in a condominium, but was talked out of it by his brother-in-law, who claimed to be a big real estate expert. Unfortunately, the brother-in-law owned a grocery store in Oregon and the purchase was in south Florida. The brother-in-law had never been to Florida. Both clients would have made a great deal of money had they made their investments, and they would have enjoyed their purchase.

Traditionally, it has been the American Dream for every American to be able to own a home. Today's market offers a variety of possibilities and the financing to go with it. The worst investment is, more often than not, the investment you don't make.

CHAPTER 5

Buying a Resale

In the preceding chapter we observed that there are some major advantages of buying from a developer. You purchase a new property, never lived in before, and you buy it at a price that, you hope, will appreciate over time. However, we also noted that there are risks associated with this type of preconstruction purchase. Will the project be completed on schedule, or at all? Will the project turn out the way the developer advertised it? What will happen once the condominium association takes over the property? These are risks you may not wish to take. Or there may not be a new project available in the area where you wish to make your purchase. For these reasons, you may be interested in purchasing a pre-owned condo, co-op, or townhouse.

ADVANTAGES OF BUYING A RESALE

1. *You can see the finished product.* When you purchase a resale, the property already exists; you see the building and the apartment as they are. You are not relying on the representations of the developer.

2. *Possible lower price.* A resale may be less expensive than a developer's unit. However, because real estate tends to appreciate, that may not always be true. Sometimes, an existing unit in a successful project will sell at a premium.

3. *Room to negotiate.* Purchasing a resale from a private individual gives you more negotiating power than dealing with a developer, in areas of price as well as terms.

4. *Less distractions when you* ~~need it.~~ You ~~...~~

1. ~~*Problems related to the age of the building.*~~ The older the building is, the more likely it will be in need of repairs and upkeep. There may be structural deterioration requiring major repairs, or simply operating systems that need replacement, such as the building's air conditioning and electrical systems. Or the building may need renovating, such as painting the exterior or redecorating the lobby. It is therefore critical for a buyer to inspect the building as well as the individual unit before purchasing a resale.

2. *Out-of-date buildings.* Buildings constructed years ago may be structurally sound but old-fashioned. This may not bother you personally but could affect your ability to sell in the future.

3. *Difficult to remodel.* There is only so much that cosmetically can be done to an older unit. In addition, you may have to get the board's approval prior to taking down walls, or obtain permits from the city prior to making changes that involve electricity or plumbing. Adding such items as washers and dryers may be impossible because the plumbing does not support it.

4. *Older technology.* Security and fire prevention systems may not reflect the latest technology. Also, in areas subject to storms and hurricanes, older buildings may not have the strongest and most wind- and water-intrusion-resistant glass.

WATCH THIS: A condo conversion is simply a building, usually used as a rental property, that is bought by a developer who then sells the units individually as condominiums. Some developers will maintain only the structural shell and modernize the entire internal facility, including electricity and plumbing, while others will do a cosmetic upgrade by building a fancy lobby or painting the units and replacing old appliances with newer, more modern ones. If you are buying a condo conversion, determine to what extent the developer has upgraded or modernized the building. Is it new, or does it just look new and have the same problems any 20- to 50-year-old building will have?

Ready to Move

You and your spouse are looking to move. Perhaps you desire a smaller home now that the children have moved out. Maybe you like the idea of leaving the private house and moving to a building with sports amenities, security, and services such as lawn care and valets to park your car. You've dreamed about living in the city, and you are now willing to sacrifice space for location. You are ready to purchase a condo, co-op, or townhouse.

You've considered the matter and asked yourself some hard questions. You've determined that you want to buy a resale because you need the property to be ready for immediate move-in. That is a good first step, because it eliminates one type of possible purchase. It narrows the choices. In accordance with our golden rule, the driving force for the decision should be which type of purchase represents the best real estate investment that you can afford. The only way to determine that is to become familiar with the area's real estate market, even if it is close to home but especially if you are moving to a new location.

TEACHING POINT: You may think you know your own area's real estate market, but you must still do the research. You may be surprised at the results you find when you actually begin to investigate the resales based on specific data.

Setting a Price Range

First, you should establish the parameters of your search, especially the price. Sometimes sales representatives will ask your price range, but many times they won't and will show you the most expensive property they have. You might assume they do this to try and sell the most expensive property they have, thereby maximizing their commission. This could be true but is not usually a primary factor with experienced salespeople. Experienced salespeople will assume that whatever price is given by prospects is what they would like to spend but is not necessarily what they *can* spend if they see something they like. Usually, they can afford more than they disclose.

The good salesperson realizes this if you give a higher

price limit. In many cases, a purchaser doesn't know area prices and stating a figure may not be useful. You may be shocked at the figure (known in the trade as *sticker shock*) but you should not be put off.

BEGINNING YOUR SEARCH

There are several ways to begin your search for resale property. Here are three useful tips:

1. *Check the local newspaper in the area you desire.* Most local newspapers have a real estate supplement. Many are in the Sunday paper but some have special weekly supplements as well. Look for well-written, informative advertisements that give prices and specific locations, so you can check them first. General ads such as "Great Apartment for sale, call Ed" tell you nothing and should be avoided. There is also a safety factor here. Remember that you are going to visit the units and you know nothing about the people who placed the ad. On a first visit, it may be prudent to take a friend with you.

2. *Consult local area Realtors.* Using a qualified professional is the safest and best way to obtain a total picture of the area you are researching. Also, a Realtor can suggest alternatives if what you initially wanted is beyond your price range. For example, you may have wanted a condo in the City Center, but you find it to be unaffordable. However, a co-op in the same area is affordable, and you may wish to make the alternative purchase.

3. *Check your credit.* We have already discussed this in previous chapters. However, in the case of a resale, the sellers are generally not real estate developers or professional investors and may want to see a prequalification letter. As indicated earlier, it is no guarantee that you will obtain financing, but at least it puts the seller at ease that, other factors being equal, you can obtain financing and they will be more comfortable taking their property off the market while the financing process is being completed.

QUESTIONS TO ASK

Regardless of whether you use a Realtor, you will still need to think about and ask many questions and do your A.P.E. research. What questions do you need to ask?

1. *Is the size suitable?* Let's say you have seen a unit of approximately 2,000 square feet. So you now have a figure to gauge space. If this size seems to work, you can proceed with your search based on this number. This may seem obvious, but many people have no idea what it means to relocate from a private house with lots of space to an apartment or townhouse where space becomes a premium. You now have a baseline for your search.

2. *Are there hidden costs?* You are told the maintenance cost is $250, which seems reasonable. It includes lawn care and the security. But what about other costs? It may turn out that the golf course membership is $15,000 per year and there is an additional monthly fee. There may be a variety of other programs including social memberships that don't allow you to play free but give you access to the restaurant. There is a minimum eating fee in addition to the social membership fee. The health and tennis club may also be additional.

3. *What's in the fine print?* If you are thinking about a golf and tennis club, who owns the amenities? Often, there are signs about, indicating that the amenities are owned by private corporations, not the association, and are open to the public and require expensive memberships. On the one hand, this may not be bad, because it can be a great expense for an association to maintain a golf course. On the other hand, what happens if the private corporation fails to properly maintain the golf course or sells the golf course to another developer who builds a high-rise apartment, and

your beautiful golf course views disappear? Not only will this affect your
quality of life and enjoyment of the property, it would affect the resale
value of your property. While this may not be likely, you should ask the
questions anyway.

about swimming pools and gymnasiums? Are these the property of the association, or are they leased? Recreation leases are not favored, and most associations, if possible, elect to purchase the property from the lessors. This results
in additional charges to the association members until such time as the
purchase is paid off. This should be disclosed by the seller, but if not, it is
up to you to ask the questions and, perhaps, check the budget carefully.
Such items will be revealed there.

6. *Is the association anticipating any major renovations that will result in special assessments?* This question is self explanatory.

TEACHING POINT: Remember, older properties may require more
care. So be sure and ask this question, even if you forget some of
the others.

7. *What is the parking situation?* How many cars can you park? Is your
parking space deeded or assigned?

TIPS ON PARKING: Parking spaces in condos are either "assigned" or
"deeded." A *deeded* parking space is real estate. You own it and can
sell or rent it as you desire. An *assigned* parking space is a limited
common element. It does not belong to you but rather to the
association. You have exclusive rights to use that spot, but the association can assign you another spot. Most parking spaces are assigned and associations rarely exercise their right to change them.
The original developer usually assigned spaces based upon the
prices of the condos. The more the original buyer paid, the better
the spot. However, parking spaces are sometimes negotiable, so

always check the location of the parking space as part of your research.

RESEARCHING THE PRICING

Here is when a broker is at his or her most valuable, if you know what to ask for.

1. Ask the broker for a printout of other similar units that have sold in the building or project you are researching. The details need not be older than six months.

2. Ask the broker for a printout of what those sellers originally paid for their property.

3. Ask the broker for a printout of similar units that are still available for sale in the building or project you are considering. Again, you need not go back more than six months. These details will give you an idea of the comparatives or *comps* for the property you are researching.

Comparative Sales: The Comps

The *comps* on what is currently listed for sale will give an indication of what people are hoping to receive for their property, while closed sales or *solds* give a realistic view of what has actually been achieved in terms of sales prices. Taking the two into consideration should give you a good indication of what price to offer.

There are exceptions. In a robust real estate market, where there is low supply and high demand, the solds data may not be an accurate reflection of the increasing appreciation in the market. Where the market has fallen, high prices reflected in the solds data may not reflect current conditions. For example, a prominent developer announces a new luxury project next to a building where there were few sales and the prices were stagnant. All of a sudden, this formerly stagnant building becomes a "hot property" and there is great demand for the few units that are on the market. Prices rise quickly, but as there are few existing sales; it takes time for the research to reflect the new higher prices based on the changed conditions.

An example in reverse is a building that, under its rules, allows for a very liberal rental policy that brings in a good return for the owner/landlords. Disgusted with the transient tenants, the board of directors, all of whom are full-time residents, pass a very harsh set of rules that no longer allow for rentals for less than one year or dogs over 20 pounds, and new purchasers require that at least one party to the deed is over 55 years of age. On top of those new restrictions, the in

Real Estate War Story 1. Several years ago, we owned a property in South America. It was a beautiful condominium located in the heart of the nation's capital. We didn't rent the apartment because the apartment was so cheap to keep in dollars that it didn't matter. The real estate market in that country was robust and the apartment was appreciating in value. Although we rarely used it, it was close to our family, and when we did travel, we enjoyed staying there. However, we began to get disturbing rumors about property values lowering, due to political changes in government policies. Finally, we decided to list the property for sale and did so based on the market value of the property, which was still high. Unfortunately for us, the property did not sell quickly.

After a few months on the market, our broker in South America advised us to lower the price because the overall economy had slowed down and the real estate market cooled. We didn't listen. We knew the last four similar properties in that area had sold at or about the price at which we had listed our unit and we weren't going to lower the price because the local broker was getting impatient. When we finally made a trip to South America, we saw that the broker was right and the market had changed. Rather than give the property away, we effectuated a suitable rental and held the property until the market recovered. We then sold it at a profit.

TEACHING POINT: The moral of the story is that if you own property, you cannot gauge your actions, whether buying or selling, simply on what the last sale may have commanded. The comps are but one indication of price.

Real Estate War Story 2. We recently purchased a condominium in south Florida as an investment property. The unit was in terrible condition and needed substantial renovation. However, the area and the community in general was enjoying a renaissance and prices were going up. We purchased a choice unit with comparatively large square footage, great floor plan, and views from every room. Even after negotiating the price, we still paid one of the highest prices to that date in that community. On top of that, we spent significant investment dollars to upgrade the unit to a high standard for that community. Everyone thought we were crazy. However, the community continued to increase in value, and within a short time several other similar unimproved units sold at even higher prices than we had paid. We had no longer paid the most for a property in that community. This is an example where the economy and the analysis of the specific community overrode negotiations based on the comps.

Interpreting the Results

Let's examine some sample comp results to see how this helps you price a property. Suppose that there have been eight sales of comparable units during the past six months. The original developer prices of the eight properties varied from about $130,000 to $165,000 when purchased five years ago. The average price of the recent resales was around $320,000, although the highest price at $440,000 slightly skewed the average. The properties were on the market for about two to three months prior to being sold, although the one property, which sold for $440,000, had been on the market about six months. Apparently, the story went that it was a beautifully furnished corner unit on the golf course. It had every upgrade and electronic device in the world, and the buyers fell in love with it. The joke among the brokers was that the buyers paid $100,000 for $10,000 of gadgets. We'll talk more about this in Chapter 10 on selling your property.

Now we'll look at a fact sheet on the specific property that you are thinking about purchasing. You discover that the seller bought the property new from the developer three years ago for a price of $155,000. The property has been on the market for one month. The broker indicates there has been interest in the property but no offers. The seller is asking $335,000.

Is This a Good Deal?

What do you think, is this a good real estate investment? What price should you offer, or should you walk away? What facts do we have? On the positive side, you are moving from a private home and will be downsizing. Although condos and townhouses will probably not provide you with the space you had in a private home, the community you have chosen is growing and appears to be the best in the area. It is close to the city and shopping, secure and with excellent amenities. Also, the project offers ample parking.

... there is also the issue of fixing the property. It needs a paint job and some new appliances.

Before making the offer, you should ask to see the property again. Check for cracks and leaks. Check the appliances. Take another walk around the property.

PROFESSIONAL INSPECTIONS: Most contracts allow for professional inspections. A professional inspection by a certified inspector is usually around $150. This is something that should always be done by the buyer when purchasing a resale, and the sale should be subject to a successful inspection. We will talk more about this in Chapter 7 when we discuss contracts.

Buyer's Market or Seller's Market?

Related to the comps, there are two terms we need to discuss. These are the *buyer's market* and the *seller's market*. When negotiating real estate you will hear these terms a lot, and they are conceptually simple. A buyer's market occurs when there is more supply than demand. As a consequence, those willing to buy have a greater negotiating posture. A seller's market is the reverse, where there is a great deal of demand and less inventory available. In this case, the sellers exercise greater authority and command a higher price and a faster sale than would be revealed by the comps. Because of the short supply, buyers have to pay a premium to purchase property.

Some brokers apply the terms *buyer's* and *seller's* markets to specific properties. We have seen advertisements for specific buildings that claim that it is a buyer's or seller's market for that property. While not a technically incorrect use of the terms, buyer's and seller's markets should be thought of as simple bell curves that usually reflect the overall or general market conditions of an area as a whole. Sometimes, governments influence buyer's and seller's markets when they adjust the interest rates. Obviously, there are many other general economic factors as well, such as consumer confidence, unemployment, the price of oil, and so on. However, local factors are important, too. For example, you buy a condominium near a ski resort. Shortly after the purchase, there is a giant avalanche and several houses are damaged. This could have a chilling effect on prices in the area. Usually, these effects are temporary.

Other Information to Consider

Returning to your situation, the comps indicate a certain price range for resale housing in the community where you are making the offer. Are we missing any fact? The answer is yes. Can you guess what additional information you should have? The answer is that you should also know what the price of the developer's new home sales are. This will provide added information on the overall market value.

What can a similar new home command? Let's say that a 3,000-square-foot townhouse bought from the developer starts at around $400,000, a little bit more than resale units but not terribly more. Looking at the comps, it appears that the community is appreciating well and prices are holding. Although resale prices are being kept somewhat suppressed because the developer is still offering new units at competitive prices, sellers are not giving away their property either, and a property on the market for two to three months is a relatively short time for a sale. In addition, the average sales price is fairly close to the average list price, which means that the sellers are getting pretty close to their asking price.

The message to you is that this is a stable community that is developing nicely. The people who are willing to sell this particular townhouse are not willing to wait three months for a sale. Perhaps they need the money for another investment or are just impatient or unhappy with the community. Whatever the reason, they were apparently willing to accept an aggressive offer for a quick sale.

TEACHING POINT: Many buyers ask the broker why the seller wants to sell. In most cases, it doesn't pay to ask because no broker or seller is going to say, "They really need the money, they're desperate." or, "They're selling because they hate it."

What other facts could you discover before making an offer? Can you think of anything else? What about the mortgage? The broker can give you a copy of the public record tax roll, which will indicate if there is a mortgage on the property. If the seller has too big a mortgage, or no mortgage, that may affect the sale as well. This will be discussed in greater detail in Chapter 8 on mortgages. Should you consider whether ~~~ ~~ ~~ ~~

~~~~~~g p~~~~ ~~ ~~~ ~~g~~~~~~~~. ~~~~ are misconceptions. There is no legal obligation for a seller to make a counter offer. In many cases, a seller will be insulted by a lowball offer and refuse to continue the negotiation, thereby forcing the buyer to either abandon the transaction or make a new offer closer to the seller's asking price. In this way, the position of the buyer becomes weaker, not stronger, and he or she has gained no information but, rather, has antagonized the seller.

INSPECTION AND RESCISSION PERIODS

Some states' laws require a rescission period in certain real estate transactions where a community association is involved. The purpose of the rescission period is to give the buyer a chance to study the association documents before making a final commitment. In Florida, for example, if one purchases a condominium directly from a developer, there is a two-week rescission period. However, if one purchases a resale condominium, there is a three-day rescission period. These rescission periods can vary, depending on what type of property you buy, or there may not be a rescission period.

TEACHING POINT: You should always check to make sure if you have any rescission periods with regard to your real estate transaction. Consult with your broker or lawyer, or you can call the local board of Realtors.

In most cases, the real estate contracts will contain a clause allowing the purchaser to have the property inspected by a certified inspector. Some contracts give the purchaser the right to withdraw from a contract if for any reason that purchaser is not satisfied with the inspection. Often, no specific reason need be stated to the seller. Most contracts require the seller to be given the opportunity to cure any defects the inspector finds, or challenge the findings of the buyer's inspector. Inspections usually take place within 10 days of the effective date of the contract.

In most cases, the purchaser is also entitled to a *walk-through* prior to the closing of the property to ascertain that he or she is receiving it in the condition that it was contracted for. However, unless there is a material change in the condition of the property, the buyer needs to close.

With a resale, the purchaser has somewhat more leverage to negotiate costs. Surveys of the property, inspections, environmental studies, if necessary, are usually borne by the purchaser. The seller is interested only in selling his or her property. It is up to the buyer to decide what investigations he or she wishes to perform.

Most states require full disclosure of any facts that might affect the value or marketability of the project. Other states follow the principal of *caveat emptor*—let the buyer beware. In other words, it is up to the buyer to investigate his or her purchase, and the seller has no duty to disclose anything negative about the property. Even in *full disclosure* states, it is imperative, when purchasing a resale, to do a full inspection of the property. Once again, state law controls what type of license an inspector will require. In some states, anyone can call himself or herself an inspector, while in others, they must be regulated in accordance with state law.

USING A BROKER

The other issue we need to discuss is the use of real estate brokers. As we stated earlier, real estate brokers are a valuable resource. A good real estate broker can provide the type of experience or information on a property that you could not acquire by ordinary research methodology. As in any other profession, there are good and honest brokers and those with less than sterling qualities or skills. It is up to you to choose the right one. This is done with the same care and research you would choose a doctor, attorney, or accountant.

Check the background and credentials of a real estate broker before you retain him or her. Many people see a big office or a multistate or multinational real estate company and automatically assume the broker is competent. This should not be assumed. Most brokers are independent contractors. This means they "hang their license" with a brokerage firm but are practically self-employed. Some even rent desk space from an agency and have very little ties with the actual broker. You could have the best broker in the world who works for a small company, or conversely, the worst broker who happens to have placed his license with a large

————— always paid by the seller. Some people are uncomfortable with that, for several reasons. The first is they feel that the *fiduciary relationship* or loyalty of the broker will always be to the person paying the commission. The second is that prospects always assume that they can negotiate a better deal if there is no commission involved so they try to work without a broker. This is tied to a third misconception, that the prospect knows more about the subject than the professional. Let's deal with those three points.

The first is the issue of the *commission*. Although a broker's commission is paid by the seller, most states have rules regarding disclosure of the fiduciary relationship of the broker. Thus, it is entirely possible that a broker may actually be representing both parties. This is often known as a "transaction broker" and must be disclosed to both parties at the onset of the transaction. A broker acts as a transaction broker when the broker has the listed property of the seller and then finds a purchaser whom he or she will also represent. Transaction brokering is not a conflict of interest if handled properly by the broker. In some cases, the broker does not have a property listing that the purchaser wishes to buy and will locate a suitable property listed with another real estate broker. In this situation, the buyer's broker acts on behalf of the purchaser and the seller's broker works on behalf of his or her seller. Brokers owe their clients their respective fiduciary loyalty even though the buyer's broker gets his or her commission from the seller.

The second issue that deserves a comment is the misconception that a person can better negotiate his or her real estate transaction without a broker because there is no commission involved. From the buyer's perspective, it is wrong because the buyer assumes that any savings would be passed on to the buyer rather than being retained by the seller. In fact, the seller wants his or her price, regardless of the commission. If the seller were to save on the commission, he or she would retain it rather than pass it along. The seller is not a charitable institution, either. Sellers often feel they can do the same job as a broker by simply placing an ad in the paper and waiting for the right buyer to come. As we shall see in Chapter 10, it is far more complicated than that. Basically, you get what you pay for. Get the best broker you can and you will get the most benefit. But you can't nor should you simply rely on the broker, you always need to be involved and knowledgeable yourself.

The third issue involves the assumption that a purchaser is better off without a broker. As we have said, a good broker is an invaluable research tool both in the purchase or sale of a property. Good brokers should have information on developers, buildings, prices, and mortgages, and should be able to help you with the effectuation of the transaction. However, as previously noted, many people feel they know more than the professional. We firmly believe that people should participate in whatever they are doing that affects their personal or professional lives. Thus, a person should participate in his or her health plans with their doctors, or legal matters with their lawyers, or taxes with their accountants. We would never advocate putting blind trust in anyone—hence this book, which you are reading and hopefully learning from. By the same token, there is no substitute for experience, and professionals, by virtue of their education and experience, should be able to provide you with superior knowledge that should enable you to make an informed decision on whatever matter you are dealing with.

My wife and I have been working in real estate for over 25 years. The plain fact is that we know more about real estate than an engineer who has spent the past 25 years designing computers or a doctor treating patients. For them, and for other professionals in different fields, using a qualified broker should result in making a better investment.

Is the Property Right for You?

We have stressed that our golden rule is that a real estate purchase is always an investment and one should view it with a certain amount of dispassionate objectivity. However, it should also be something you like. The two are not mutually exclusive. If you like a property but it is a bad investment on paper, you should pass it by. Likewise, if it is a great investment but you hate it, it may not be worth buying even if you have absolutely no intention of ever using it personally.

With most properties, you are going to incur expenses. You may need to furnish them, or repair them. If you like what you bought, you are more likely to want to invest in it. Real estate is fun and exciting. You can be creative in working with the property. Therefore, it will be much easier if

DOWNSIZING

Many people move from large homes to apartments. Their children move out and they no longer need a large house. But what about all their belongings? When Nora and I first got married, we furnished our new apartment. One of the objects we splurged on was an Italian dining room table. It was quite large, but worked for that apartment. A couple of years later we sold our apartment (a condominium). Of course, we took the table, but it didn't look right in our new home, which was a bit smaller. Over the years, one of our considerations in making real estate purchases that we were going to live in was whether or not the table would fit. It was like it was part of our family. Finally, we sold our apartment and gave the table to the new owner as part of the sale. Upon reflection, we realized that we had spent a fortune carting that table all over the world, only to give it away at the end.

It is part of human nature to develop attachments to inanimate objects. Old shoes, furniture, books, jewelry, the list is endless. That's normal. Objects carry memories for people. They are souvenirs of their lives. But when these objects take over one's decision making, when their existence begins to interfere with what, in good common sense, ought to be the right decision, when things become more important than people and when these objects, in effect, dictate how people run their lives, it is perhaps time to take stock by disposing of them. In other words, it is time to throw things out.

Physics teaches us that two solid objects cannot occupy the same space at the same time. Consequently, one cannot fit objects that occupied a 5,000-square-foot house in a 2,000-square-foot apartment. If you are moving to a condominium from a house, that's great. Get rid of your "stuff" and buy the condominium. That is a decision you should make up front, and your search for real estate should be directed by that decision. It is fruitless to look at condominiums when you have spent the past 20-odd years in a large house and then try to reconcile moving all of your life into the smaller investment. To do so often leads to frustration because what you wind up purchasing is an expensive warehouse for your furniture, and that is usually the wrong investment. If you want to change your lifestyle, that change has to begin with a commitment to find the investment you want, and you must accept the consequences of that decision. Throwing things out only hurts for a little while.

Thus far, you have seen in general terms, the transactions involved in the purchase of a condominium directly from a developer, and a resale. In Chapter 7, we get to the specifics of the transaction, the paperwork. In particular, we will examine the contract for sale, the condominium documents, and the closing statement. But first, let's examine the relationship you're entering into. With the kinds of properties discussed in this book, you will be dealing with associations representing your fellow owners and those associations' boards of directors.

CHAPTER 6

Dealing with the Board of Directors

Community associations, whether they are for condos, cooperatives, or townhouses that belong to a homeowners association, have one thing in common—they are governed by boards of directors. Dealing with these boards may present some unique and interesting problems. In this chapter, we will tell you what to expect and how to interact with your board. Perhaps you may even wish to be part of one.

Boards of directors are elected in accordance with the association's documents. The entire board may run for election at one time or the elections of members may be staggered so there will always be previously elected board members serving. Election rules are governed by state laws and your association documents. In most cases, the entire board runs for reelection each year.

Boards of directors are generally not professional managers but tend to be concerned members of the association who want to contribute their time to help run their respective associations. Many are retired businesspeople. In many, if not most cases, the members have no prior experience in running a condominium or other association. Unless specifically provided for in the association's governing documents, board members are not compensated. Serving on the board is strictly volunteer work. Ironically, this is one of the few situations where people with little or no past experience are literally put in charge of millions of dollars in cash and property. They often control not only your enjoyment of your property, but also the future of your real estate investment.

POWERS OF THE BOARD

The powers of a board of directors are enumerated in the association's documents. Generally, they are given sufficient powers to operate and manage the association. They can open bank accounts for the association, enter into contracts for services on behalf of the association, appoint committees to assist them, and collect maintenance to support the various projects that maintain the community—such as managers, maintenance staff, security, and valet services, to name a few. They are also charged with preparing a budget and operating within that budget to the greatest degree possible. However, they can also raise funds when necessary by calling for special assessments for needed but unfunded repairs and improvements. As required, they must also pass rules and regulations for the members to follow.

Most states have specific statutes that govern how a board must operate, how often they must call meetings of the membership, and what the limits of their powers are. Where the association documents conflict with state law, state law governs. Because many board members are not experienced, it often falls upon the property manager to help and guide the board. Also, the association's lawyers are of great value in this regard.

A board of directors can make or break an association. If properly managed, the project can run smoothly and the fees kept as low as possible. However, a poor board can cause grave problems, just as with any other poorly managed operation. This can include degradation of the building due to poor maintenance, high monthly fees and frequent special assessments, and a general devaluation of your investment.

YOUR FIRST ENCOUNTER WITH THE BOARD

Usually, your first encounter with a board of directors will be at the initial interview, when you purchase a resale unit. Developers serve as board directors until the unit reaches a certain occupancy rate determined by state law, so buying directly from a developer generally does not involve any board interviews.

We have already noted in earlier chapters that the type of association will determine how much power a board of directors has. Condominiums and homeowners associations generally have less power than cooperative boards.

When purchasing a resale, you will most likely be given an information packet to fill out. Depending on the association, some of these questions

erty owner or tenant, and even try to determine your net worth.

The association may also wish to know if you are a threat to the other residents. In Dade County, Florida, a new law requires brokers who sell a unit to a family with children under a certain age to contact the police to determine if there are any convicted child abusers living within a certain prescribed distance from the new buyers.

Most of these questions are legitimate in terms of a background check, although I usually draw the line at submitting tax returns. Tax returns are personal, and most financial information that the board needs can be verified through credit checks. Boards don't need tax returns to determine creditworthiness. Thus far, I have not been challenged when I refuse to submit tax returns, either personally, or on behalf of a client.

TEACHING POINT: My advice is to answer the questions truthfully and supply as much information as you feel necessary to prove your worthiness to live in the building. If you feel that the board is going too far, consult with your attorney before filling out the form, or simply tell the board that you don't wish to answer that question or provide the requested document and discuss the matter with them or the property manager.

The Interview

Many boards require a personal interview, along with the application form. Most times, this is merely a chance to meet and welcome a new unit owner, and it gives the board the opportunity to discuss the rules and regulations of the association with the new owner. However, some boards are more aggressive and even threatening. Take this with a grain of salt. Remember, you can vote for or against these people once you are an owner, or you can eventually run for the board yourself.

The idea is to get past this hurdle. Be polite and answer questions honestly and forthrightly. A board interview is not the time to fight. The ability to pay maintenance, taxes, and expenses, your general creditworthiness, and any past criminal activity may be criteria for judging whether to approve a contract. However, a board cannot discriminate based on race, creed, color, or national origin. If you feel that you were wrongly turned down by a board, you should consult an attorney.

TEACHING POINT: Allow sufficient time in the closing process for the board interview. Often, a board member or members may be on vacation or otherwise unavailable to conduct the interview. They may not care about, or simply be unable to accommodate your closing date and will conduct interviews according to their own schedules. It pays to set up your interview well in advance of your closing so there won't be any problems with the closing date stipulated in the contract. Most real estate transactions that require board approval cannot be finalized until the closing agent receives an official letter from the board indicating that you have been approved.

Typical Questions

Most board members will have reviewed your application and results of the credit check. If everything is in order, the questions should be pretty general. They will ask whether you plan to be a permanent or part-time resident. Often, they'll ask about your job. If you are a professional such as a doctor, accountant, or lawyer, or sell a popular product such as cars, computers, or real estate, be prepared to be asked to give some free advice. You may also be asked to volunteer your services. Even if you have no intention of doing so, be polite and say you will certainly consider it.

TEACHING POINT: An interview is not always a one-way conversation. You can also ask questions—and you should. Ask about the budget: Are there any new special assessments looming? Ask board members if there are any structural problems, if there are reserve emergency funds, and if there are any other concerns that you should be aware of. You may want to know about the rules concerning moving in, or having guests or noisy neighbors. Ask if there is a judicial committee that hears complaints or enforces the rules. Show them you care about being a good owner.

Getting Involved in the Association

Attending these meetings can be quite an experience either positively or negatively, depending on how the meetings are conducted. Over the years we've attended very civil and professional meetings—and we have attended meetings where fistfights erupted and security guards had to be posted. One memorable fight occurred between an older gentleman and a young fellow. The young fellow was lean and muscular and very opinionated. The older gentleman was equally opinionated, and the two got into a heated discussion about some issue concerning noise at the swimming pool. As the argument became more heated, the young fellow took a swing at the older man, who happened to be an ex-Army Ranger. The old fellow quickly overpowered the young man, much to the young man's astonishment and embarrassment. While amusing, this is not the way to conduct meetings. But it happens. Hopefully, it won't happen in your case. Such occurrences are usually indicative of a weak board that cannot control its meetings.

Attending the meetings is important because it is how you know what is going on in the building. It also serves to introduce you to your neighbors and your board of directors. Members of the board are usually not compensated and usually serve out of a sense of duty. They are obligated to run the condominium in accordance with state law and condominium documents. If you have a problem that you cannot resolve at the building manager's level, this is the place to discuss it. In a new project, the first few meetings are generally well attended, and then interest fades unless there is some major problem, such as a special assessment. Then everyone attends the meeting to find out the particulars, until once again interest fades. It is not necessary to attend each and every board meeting, but you should go to at least one just to get a feel for the place you are going to live in.

Should You Run for the Board?

Another question that arises is, should you, as an owner, run for the board? The answer is, it depends on you and your personality. The best board members are generally retired professional people such as lawyers and accountants. They understand the law and numbers and have the time to devote to the affairs of the building. People who already have full-time jobs or careers that call for extensive travel won't have the time necessary to devote to the building. It can also be a high-stress job.

One of the best board presidents I have ever seen was a retired businessman who served on the board of the condominium we lived in, practically until his death. Each day you would find him around the building or the manager's office, making sure everything was proceeding smoothly. He was very tough, and even when we crossed swords, in retrospect, he was usually right. Those are the kind of people you want running your building.

We have had people say to us, "We don't want any rules. This is our building and we should be able to do what we want; it shouldn't be run like a prison." In one particular instance, the board of directors agreed and rarely enforced any rules. Of course, the person most vocal in wanting no rules was the first to complain and be outraged when his neighbor hired a Mariachi band for some occasion and the festivities began at 1:00 A.M. on a weeknight.

We recently attended the turnover meeting of our new condominium. A *turnover meeting* occurs in accordance with state laws that require that the developer "turn over" control of the association to the unit owners when a certain percentage of units are sold. Our condominium documents called for a three-member board. Six or seven people ran for the three seats. None of the candidates who submitted resumes had any prior experience in sitting on a condominium board of directors, although all had general business experience. One member was a retired businessman. Of the six candidates, two of the three elected were not present at the meeting, and only the retired person attended; it was evident that few understood much about their investment or how a condominium operates. Although it is too early to tell how this new board will perform, it is clear that both the owners and the board members are going to be in for a long educational process.

Of major concern to the membership was the fact that the lounge chairs at the pool did not recline. Although this may be of legitimate concern, it ranks low on a new board's list of priorities. One unit owner was so upset over the fact that the pool chairs didn't recline that he suggested, quite seriously, that the owners throw them into the ocean. Oddly enough, this suggestion seemed to garner much support among those listening. Aside from

their monthly maintenance. Association members should be prepared for this and should budget for it at the onset. If it happens, it is to be expected—if not, welcome it as a pleasant surprise. The average increase is usually about 10 percent to 15 percent, although that can vary greatly, depending on how much the developer underestimated the carrying costs. Generally speaking, the appreciation of the investment in the property will more than compensate for any initial aggravations.

CHOOSE YOUR BATTLES

Most people live in peace and enjoy their condominium investments, while others spend their lives fighting. The question becomes, when do you fight and when do you hold your peace?

Since we treat every real estate purchase as an investment, we were generally very active in our associations, often in director or managerial roles. Quite frankly, if I had to do it again, I would pass on both roles. They are thankless positions. Fortunately, there are people who like to serve as directors or manage buildings. More power to them.

My advice is to choose your battles wisely. My gauge for fighting is if I perceive that the board is doing something that places my investment in *serious jeopardy*. Let's look at some examples.

Let us suppose that the board of directors passes a rule forbidding dogs in the building. Will such a rule jeopardize my investment? Possibly, because if dogs are forbidden in the building, it decreases the pool of people who may consider purchasing or leasing my apartment. But does it place my investment in *serious* jeopardy? The answer is no! While it is true that dog owners can no longer consider buying my unit, there are still plenty of people who don't own dogs who might want to live in a pet-free environment. The fact that the building will no longer allow pets does not destroy the value of my investment.

What about a rule that abolishes rentals, and you purchased your condominium as a rental property. That rule has serious immediate and long-term repercussions. The immediate repercussions are that you can no longer derive income from you property. If you depend on the income from the rentals to defray the cost of your mortgage, you could have a very bad, immediate problem with your bank. Fortunately, if the condominium documents provide for renting the property, the documents would have to be amended in order to put such a rule into effect.

Most condominium documents require a two-thirds vote of the membership be present at a meeting and vote affirmatively in order to legally make such an amendment. It is next to impossible to get two-thirds of the membership to show up at board meetings, let alone agree to such an amendment, so the likelihood that such an amendment would take place is very small. However, in such a case, this would be a battle that you would want to be involved in. Even if you were not leasing your unit, a rental restriction tends to lower the value of the apartments.

Some Final Thoughts on Boards

Boards of directors are governed by laws. First, and foremost, they must obey any and all federal and state laws. Second, they must obey the dictates of their governing documents. The most important aspect of an effective board is that it be concerned with the welfare of the association's members and their property.

An owner should not sit on the board simply because he or she has a strictly personal agenda to advance, or as an ego booster, or because he or she is retired and misses the action, or because this is the opportunity to be the "boss" he or she never was.

Equally important is that board members should be full-time residents who have the time to serve. Absentee members who live elsewhere, or those with demanding jobs who cannot devote the time necessary to being a board member, and who merely show up for the meetings, if they even bother to do that, cannot be effective.

If you feel that your board is not effective, you should attend the board meetings and ask questions in accordance with your rights as a member. But don't be disruptive. Most meetings are conducted in accordance with state law and *Robert's Rules of Order.* State your issue clearly and briefly, listen to the response, and sit down. If you are not satisfied and you feel your rights are being violated, consult an attorney. Some states have agencies that deal with or regulate community association boards, and they may

CHAPTER 7

Understanding the Paperwork

Thus far, I've tried to give you a feel for what you will encounter when you begin the process of purchasing a property that involves a community association. However, selecting property, making an offer, getting it accepted, and being approved is only half the battle. Of equal importance is the ability to understand the process, which is reflected in the considerable paperwork involved. This is something you should understand. As you will see, brokers and attorneys are useful—in some cases, essential—but when it comes to the paperwork, there is no substitute for personal knowledge in effectuating a real estate transaction. You need to have a basic understanding of the transaction, and in the case of real estate, this is exemplified in the paperwork.

In this chapter we will discuss the contract, condominium association documents, and the HUD closing statement. These are essential ingredients in the purchase of a community association type of property. In the next chapter on financing, we will discuss the mortgage documents, which are the other essential pieces of paperwork. Unfortunately, there is no way to liven up the presentation. It is just a matter of going through the various documents and explaining how to read and understand them and what you should be on the lookout for. Some of the issues have already been touched on in the previous chapters so they will not be entirely new.

THE CONTRACT

We will begin our discussion of the paperwork with the first document you will encounter in the real estate transaction, the *contract*. The contract is the blueprint for

there must be *consideration*. Technically, to have valid consideration, each party to the contract must have an added burden placed on him or herself as a result of becoming a party to the contract.

Valid consideration does not necessarily involve money. For example, let's say Owner Tom enters into a contract with Broker Patty to sell his home. The contract stipulates that Tom must now make the home available for showing by Patty, and Patty must make her best efforts to sell the home, which may include advertising it on the Web or broker listing network. The contract places a new burden on each participant, although money has not been exchanged.

However, in today's standard agreements, money is the medium for valid consideration. It does not have to be a great deal of money. For example, you may often see the phrase "$10.00 and other valuable consideration." This is a token phrase acknowledging that the contract bears valid consideration.

Contracts also must have a definite beginning and termination date to be valid. Often you will see self-renewing contracts that seem to go on forever. In fact, the terms usually state that the contract will renew if neither party terminates by a specific date. This is construed as an automatic renewal of the contract rather than a contract with no definitive end.

Contracts are either *bilateral* or *unilateral*. This simply means that contracts can have two parties or one party to the agreement. For example, you receive a postcard from a department store that states that if you come on a certain date and between certain hours, you will receive a 20 percent discount on all purchases over $100. This is a unilateral contract. You are not obligated to come to the store or make any purchases, but the store has placed a burden upon itself to give a discount where it had no such prior obligation.

A bilateral contract is a two-party contract. This is the standard type of agreement we are all familiar with. A real estate contract is a bilateral agreement. It has two parties, the buyer and the seller. The seller, whether a developer or an owner on the resale market, offers the property at a desired price. The buyer, the second party to the agreement, either accepts the seller's offer or makes a counteroffer at a price he or she wishes to establish.

KEY POINT: A *counteroffer* is not an acceptance of a contract. Thus, if the *offeror* offers to sell his or her property for $400,000 and the buyer, the *offeree,* counters at $325,000, there is no binding contract until the two parties agree on a price—that is, there is an offer and an acceptance.

Meeting of the Minds

There is a concept that we should discuss, known as the *meeting of the minds.* In order for there to be a valid offer and acceptance, the seller and the buyer must have agreement on what they are contracting for. The classic case involves a contract between a shipper and purchaser of goods. The shipper had two ships with the same name. The shipper thought the goods were to be shipped on ship A while the purchaser thought his goods would be coming on ship B, which arrived much earlier. The shipper demanded payment for the goods while the purchaser refused, stating that his goods arrived late and that the shipper had thus breached his contract. The court ruled that there was no meeting of the minds as to the terms of the contract—that is, which ship was to be used—and the contract was thus void.

A *voided* contract has the effect of nullifying the contract as if it never existed. In a real estate contract, the first line after the identification of the parties usually calls for not only the address of the property, but the legal description or tax identification number of the property to avoid any misunderstanding of what is being bought and sold.

The Form of a Contract

The question arises, "Is there such a thing as an oral or unwritten contract?" The answer is a confusingly contradictory yes, but in most cases it is unenforceable. As already stated, a basic contract must have an offer, acceptance, and consideration to be valid, as long as there is a definite beginning and ending term and a meeting of the minds as to the terms of the contract. Therefore, if those criteria are present, there could be a lawful oral contract, assuming you could prove it. In the United States, by a law known as the "statute and frauds," most contracts over $500 must be in writing to be enforceable.

For our purposes, let's take it as a given that all real estate contracts will

notary seal), a writing is a writing. It can be hand-written or typed. It doesn't matter, as long as the basic requirements for a valid contract are transcribed or reduced to a writing that complies with the law.

With the advent of the Internet, it has become possible to contract over the web by clicking on the acceptance button. There are even new recognized ways of "signing" the document over the Internet. There are new web sites that claim to be able to handle all facets of the real estate transaction on the Internet, but it remains to be seen how this develops. For the time being, let's keep with the standard methodology of signing with a pen.

Basic Contract Requirements

The reason it is important to use a standardized real estate contract is to avoid ambiguities that could render the contract unenforceable, not because there is something magical about a form. Let's take a look at the important parts of a real estate contract.

Identification of the Seller. The first line of a real estate contract will identify the seller(s). The seller's name must match the name on the deed of the property to be sold. If the seller is a corporation, the person who signs the contract must have authority from the corporation to sign the contract on behalf of the corporation. The corporation must also have the right (as stated in its corporate charter) to convey property. If either of these two elements are in doubt, the seller may not be able to effectuate a sale.

Similarly, if the deed contains a husband and wife and both are alive, the husband and wife must both sign the contract. These items should be checked by your broker, attorney, or closing agent, but for now, you should understand the basics. This information is a matter of public record, and it is relatively easy to log on to the county tax rolls and find out whose names appear on the deed.

My wife and I recently purchased a property that was owned by a woman who was of advanced age and legally incompetent. Her business affairs were handled by her son, who signed the contract on her behalf as provided by a court order known as a *conservatorship*. Unfortunately, her son's authority as granted by the court did not include authority to convey real estate. Basically, it was an oversight on the court's part, but it affected his right to convey the property and had to be corrected by the court prior to closing. As you can see, great care is necessary, even with regard to the first line of the contract.

Identification of the Buyer. The second line of the contract usually identifies the buyer(s). It is important for both the buyers and sellers to understand how multiple purchasers fill in the buyer's line in the contract. For example, there is a legal difference between Bill and Sally, tenants in common, and Bill and Sally, a married couple, and Bob and Phil, tenants by the entirety.

Tenants in common is a historical legal term that, in this case, has nothing to do with renting property. It means that Bill and Sally as tenants in common would own an undivided one-half interest in a property. An *undivided interest* simply means that either Bill or Sally could someday sell his or her individual rights in the property to a third party. If Bill sells his half interest to Phil, Mary would own the property equally with Phil instead of Bill. An undivided interest specifically does *not* mean that Sally owns the bedroom and bathroom and Bill owns the playroom and garage.

Married couples, unless otherwise specifically stated, are usually presumed to own property *by the entirety*. This means that it takes both signatures to sell the property. That is why you will often find on a deed such phrases as "Bill and Sally, a married couple." This is usually a clue that it is referring to a tenancy by the entirety, but these presumptions are governed by state law.

When two or more unrelated people purchase a property, it can either be tenants in the entirety or in common, and that must be specified. Investors who are partners but are buying in their own names may wish to buy as tenants in common, in accordance with their partnership agreement.

Depending on the terms of the contract, the buyer who signs may not be the ultimate purchaser. For example, if the contract allows for *assigns,* the buyer will be allowed to transfer the contract to another party. Assignments are fairly common. Sometimes, the buyer may wish to purchase in a corporate name but hasn't formed the corporation yet. Other cases may include an investor who wishes to flip the contract to a third party prior to closing. The contract should stipulate if the original l~~~~~~~~~~~~~~~~~~~~~

~~~~~~~~~~~ ~~~~~~ resolution you are uncertain of.

Property Description. The next portion of the contract involves the legal description of the property. There will usually be a space for the postal address, followed by the legal description. This is to make sure that the buyer and the seller are talking about the same property and it is correctly described. The legal description can be ascertained from the tax rolls.

Contract Essentials. Once we have dispensed with the identification of the parties to the contract and the description of the property, we get down to the contract's essentials.

1. *Consideration.* Most contracts will have a sentence indicating that valid consideration of "$10.00 and other valuable consideration" has passed hands. This does not mean that you have to give the seller a ten-dollar bill but rather, the contract acknowledges, for technical purposes, that consideration has passed hands. As we shall now see, the contract contains ample burdens on the seller and the buyer to satisfy any issues of consideration.

2. *Personal property.* Following the legal description, there is a space for filling in the personal property included in the sale. Such items as kitchen appliances should be stated here. If the unit is being sold furnished, a detailed inventory should be attached and referenced in this space. *Fixtures* are those items that are permanently attached to the property such that they are inherently part of a property, and need not be indicated. Examples of fixtures are built-in air-conditioning units and built-in closet shelves. However, items such as light fixtures and window treatments although seeming permanently affixed, may not be "fixtures" from a legally techni-

cal standpoint. When in doubt, it is better to include an item in the inventory.

The other common essentials of the contract will be the down payment and the financing terms. Most people concentrate on the former and gloss over the latter. This is a mistake. Both are important.

3. *Down payment.* Down payments are important to sellers because they want as much money up front to cement the deal as they can get. If the buyer defaults, more often than not, the down payment is what the seller is going to keep regardless of the default clause. We'll discuss defaults later in this chapter.

Some property associations require a minimum deposit, such as 20 percent. Often, property associations will try to ensure that purchasers will be able to pay costs associated with the property ownership. A larger deposit assures that the purchasers have the capital to make the purchase and are not merely buying for *spec*, i.e., speculation, or "flipping," with no money down. Where the association does not have a say in the deposit amount, the down payment is negotiable between the buyer and the seller. Buyers often want a minimum deposit to preserve their cash holdings so they can invest with other people's money. *Other people,* in this case, generally means the lending institution.

4. *Financing terms.* Once the deposit is determined, financing details are usually indicated. Often, this paragraph of the contract tends to be ignored because financing is usually a separate issue between the purchaser and the bank. However, all contract terms have relevance, and none should be ignored.

A buyer who fails to secure financing, or who secures financing upon terms and conditions that he or she may not want, could still be liable on the contract, depending on what the financing terms of the contract stipulate. For example, let us suppose that the buyer wants to secure a loan with a maximum of 6 percent interest. The bank, however, grants him or her a loan but with 6.5 percent interest. If the contract does not specify the terms of the loan to be secured, the buyer may be forced to accept the bank's offer or be in default of the contract.

If the seller is helping to finance the deal, this is the portion of the contract where this is noted as well. Therefore, buyers should be keenly aware of what financing they are willing to live with and stipulate such in this portion of the contract. If they cannot secure the desired terms from their lending institution, the seller and the buyer understand that the deal may be terminated without penalty to the buyer.

Inspection Clauses. Most real estate contracts also provide for inspection periods. The dates for these inspections are set early on in the contract. This gives the buyer the opportunity to carefully check the property for defects. When purchasing a preconstruction condominium for example and

days of the effective date of the contract. The *effective date of a contract* is the date the last party to the contract signed. Care should be exercised in reviewing the rights under the inspection clause. Some people hire companies to inspect the property. In the case of a resale, this is generally a good idea. The cost usually ranges from about $100 to $200. The company will check the appliances and air conditioning unit, as well as perform some structural investigation, usually for evidence of water leaks.

Although many contracts go into complex details about how much each party pays for any repairs, as well as rights to dispute findings of the inspector, it is much easier to simply have a clause that allows the buyer to withdraw from the contract for any reason following the inspection or accept the contract and proceed to closing. This avoids disputes about inspection results and repairs. It is the real estate equivalent of "speak now or forever hold your peace."

TEACHING POINT: Buyers should be aware that an inspection under a contract does not mean a formal inspection with a professional inspector. If the buyer shows up for an inspection during the stipulated period afforded by the contract, turns on the oven and air conditioning, and takes no further action, the buyer has had his or her inspection rights and cannot decide just prior to closing to get a professional company to perform a second inspection.

Most non–developer real estate contracts also provide for a walk-through just prior to closing. Unlike the developer walk-through, where the developer will cure defects in construction, in a resale situation, the purpose of this walk-through is to assure the buyer that the unit is in the same condition that was stipulated in the contract. It is not an opportunity for a second full-fledged inspection.

Other Parts of the Contract. The remainder of the contract probably contains lots of fine print that parties tend to gloss over. Let's take a look at a few of these other sections. One often-overlooked paragraph concerns prorations.

1. *Prorations and special assessments.* Prorations are important because they affect how much the buyer and seller each pay at closing. For example, let us assume that the real estate taxes on a property are $1,000.00 per month and the property closes on March 31, 2006. The seller would owe taxes on the property from January 1 to March 31, 2006. The buyer who takes over the property would owe the remainder of the taxes for 2006. Thus, at the closing, the taxes are *prorated* as of the date of the closing.

The prorations clause of the contract stipulates how prorations are to be calculated. Generally speaking, it is as of the date of the closing, but it does not necessarily have to be so. For example, let's say a condominium is undergoing a special assessment. In some cases, the condominium association will demand that the seller pay the complete assessment prior to approving the sale. Sellers are within their rights to make this demand if such a provision is in the condominium documents. However, this can be prorated against the buyer. It depends on what is contained in the prorations clause of the contract.

Sometimes, a contract will stipulate that special assessments are not prorated as of the date of the closing, but rather, are determined by the amount of work done in accordance with that proration. For example, if there were a special assessment for new landscaping and the job was more than half done, then the buyer would pay the entire assessment because he or she will get the most benefit from the assessment. We do not favor this type of proration because it is often difficult to tell at what stage a special assessment is at. It is sometimes up to the property manager to make the final judgment. It is far better to make sure the prorations clause deals with all prorations, including special assessments, as of the date of closing.

2. *Default clauses.* Another important but overlooked clause of the real estate contract is the default clause. This clause deals with the rights of parties if either does not comply with the terms of the contract. The rights of the defaulted party are known in contract law as *remedies.*

In real estate contracts, there are usually two remedies available to the *defaulted* party against the *defaulting* party. The first is damages, expressed in terms of money, while the second is known as *specific performance*. The vast majority of cases involve the former. When a buyer defaults—that is, re-

ɪ ne other general remedy is known as *specific performance*. Specific performance simply means that the seller sues the buyer to force him or her to complete the transaction. This is a costly and protracted method of seeking a remedy. This type of remedy is generally employed when a property is not in demand and the buyer, for whatever reason he or she originally sought to make the purchase, has a change of mind. In this case, the seller is not interested in retaining deposit money and reselling the property, but rather in forcing the buyer to complete the transaction.

Some default clauses also stipulate the method of pursuing a disputed contract. Many require mediation as a prerequisite to further legal action and some limit the parties to binding arbitration. In the overcrowded state court systems, mediation and arbitration are methods that limit the dispute to mediators and arbitrators, who replace judges. They listen to both sides and reach a decision. Mediators try to settle the case for the disputed parties, but those parties are not bound to follow the advice of the mediator. Where binding arbitration is involved, the parties are obliged to follow the decision of the arbitrator.

The problem with these methods is that the mediator or arbitrator may not always be a lawyer. Although trained in dispute resolution, employing this method often deprives the parties of the legal expertise of a judge and the rules of evidence that govern legal disputes. There are usually greater up-front costs to pay for the mediator's/arbitrator's time. If you prefer having your day in court, you should exercise care in checking the dispute resolution portion of the contract.

3. *Destruction of property.* Other boilerplate clauses deal with destruction of the property prior to closing. Most contracts will stipulate that if the property is destroyed prior to the closing, the contract is void. Where there

is substantial damage to a property but not total destruction, the seller is given an opportunity to cure the damage or he or she may void the contract.

Clauses Based on State Law. There are other general clauses found in the real estate contract that are determined by state law. For example, rescission periods and disclosure clauses.

Rescission periods are those time periods that a buyer has to back out of the deal. For example, where properties involving community associations are involved, the buyer often may be given time to study community association documents. Typically, this may be 3 to 14 business days.

These rescission periods are mandated by state legislatures in response to high-pressure sales tactics. For example, Florida has a three-day rescission period of resales of condominiums but not freestanding houses. Contracts should stipulate if a rescission period applies to a purchase.

Caution: Buyers are advised not to make any assumptions with regard to these rescission periods and to check before signing any real estate agreement.

The other important factor that buyers and sellers should be aware of is *disclosures*. We have touched briefly on this issue, but it bears some further analysis. In business, the general rule of law is called *caveat emptor,* "let the buyer beware." Unless a state legislature changes that and passes mandatory disclosure laws, that's the same rule that applies to real estate.

Mandatory disclosure means that the seller has to disclose factors about the property that the owner knows or should know about, and that are not visible to the naked eye. Thus, in states that have disclosure laws, a seller, and in many cases, the seller's broker, must disclose any hidden defect. However, even in states that have disclosure laws, buyers should still have an inspection.

One interesting example of recent litigation involves disclosure of supernatural occurrences or haunted-house cases. It has been held by some courts that where there are documented occurrences of unexplained "supernatural events," they need to be disclosed. What about a murder? Courts have similarly held that such extraordinary events should be disclosed as well. How about someone who died of natural causes? That does not generally need to be disclosed. In states that have no mandatory disclosure rules, it is up to the buyer to perform *due diligence*—a term usually associated with commercial real estate transactions—to evaluate a property's worth.

"The *Law of the Tree*, as it's defined

Developer Contracts

Developer contracts are known in legal parlance as *contracts of adhesion*. This means that they are not subject to negotiation, and if you don't sign them as they are, you don't buy the property from a developer. In addition, most developers in the area will be using the same or similar contracts and so if you don't sign them, you don't buy property from a developer.

There are, however, certain things you can negotiate with a developer. The first is the price of the purchase. You can also negotiate the terms of the down payment, although it will probably be limited to when the payments must be made rather than the amount of the down payment. Many developers demand 20 percent of the purchase price and sometimes up to 30 percent for foreign nationals. You can also negotiate the date of the closing. Sometimes, you can also negotiate what the developer will include in its package. Items such as flooring, window treatments, or appliances may be subject to some negotiation.

In a developer contract, you should also be aware of what the developer can and cannot do with your down payment. This will be stipulated in the contract but won't be obvious. Some states regulate use of down payments by developers, others do not. For example, let us say that the developer demands a 20 percent down payment. In most cases, this money will be placed in a non–interest-bearing escrow. Some developers will give interest on the down payment as a credit toward the price at closing, and that is a nice bonus if you can get it, but don't count on it. The contract will then stipulate how the monies may be used. In many cases, the first 10 percent must be held in escrow until closing; however, the developer may use the second 10 percent for construction of the project. This means that if the developer goes bankrupt, you are assured of getting only 10 percent of your deposit back, the part held in escrow. If the developer already used the second 10 percent, all or part of that money may be lost. This is why it is crucial to know the history of your developer.

Developer contracts differ from those of resales in that they generally do not provide a paragraph for financing. Developers who sell directly to the purchasers place financing arrangements and responsibility in the hands of the purchaser.

CAUTION: If you sign a developer contract without certainty as to financing, you run the risk of losing your deposit if you cannot close the deal because you could not secure financing.

Read the Fine Print

Prior to signing any contract, both parties need to understand what they are signing, but more so with a developer contract. It can be a grave mistake to dismiss all the fine print as merely boilerplate. If there were no reason for specific language to be present in a contract, it wouldn't be there.

A good example of overconfidence happened to my wife and I when we recently invested in a new condominium. We made the purchase directly from the developer and signed the contract without really reading it very carefully. After all, we are professionals, and this contract was more or less the same developer contract that we had been dealing with for more than 20 years. We secured loan commitments from two banks. One was the institution where we did the bulk of our banking and the other was done through the developer's mortgage brokerage company. Both gave us similar rates and estimates of our closing costs, which matched our own estimate. When we came to the closing, the costs were $20,000 over the estimates.

A closer inspection of the contract indicated that the developer was within its rights to charge all of the added closing costs. Neither the banks nor we had bothered to take a close look at the contract terms. Everyone we spoke to had the same complaint, but it was too late. It was almost funny to see people come from the closing with the same shocked look on their faces that we must have had. I was upset and angry, but it was our responsibility to read and understand the terms of the contract. The fact that apparently no other lending institution bothered to properly comprehend the terms or properly estimate the closing costs didn't matter.

The issue is one that many purchasers from a developer now face, especially in Florida. Closing costs, which will be discussed later in the chapter, are costs associated with finalizing the transfer of the property from the buyer to the seller. They include recording fees and other associated expenses. In south Florida, many developers charge a flat 1.7 percent charge, which is supposed to cover these charges.

...if you are buying from a developer and there is a flat fee for closing costs, which you protest against, the salesperson will tell you that it is much cheaper for the developer to pay for closing costs. That statement is true as far as it goes. Don't assume, however, that the flat fee will cover everything, and do not assume that the bank's final estimate of closing costs is going to be low and not high when they involve a developer contract.

Resale Contracts

In a resale situation, the buyer and seller are in more of an *arm's-length agreement*. This means they are more or less on equal footing in terms of negotiating posture. Also, resale contracts, while similar in content, tend to be more balanced in protecting the rights of the buyer and the seller, while the developer contract is weighed heavily in protecting only the rights of the developer.

With a resale contract, you also need to be aware of certain other terms, which are covered since this will be the blueprint for the rest of the transaction.

The first clause usually identifies the closing date. This is the date that the buyer and seller must be prepared to transfer title to the property. The seller needs to be ready to leave the property and the buyer must be ready to pay for it. If either side is not ready to close on the specified date, it could cause a default in the contract. It is incumbent upon both parties to allow sufficient time to close.

The next clause will outline the closing costs associated with the transfer. This will be discussed at the end of the chapter.

Evidence of good title is usually next on the list. Generally speaking, the seller must provide evidence of good title, which is usually accomplished through a current title policy on the property. Title to the property is the ownership right of the seller, and a title policy is an insurance policy that indicates that a title insurance company has researched the history of the property and the insurance company will stand behind the seller's/owner's rights in the property. The buyer pays for a title search. Most lending institutions employ title companies who research and update title policies. If you are buying for cash, your broker or attorney will advise you on title insurance companies.

Professional Advice

Do you need an attorney to look over the contract before making a purchase? It is always best to have a professional look over a contract prior to signing. However, in the case of developer contracts and resale contracts for condominiums and cooperatives, if they are contracts stating that they are sanctioned by the local realtor association, it is often sufficient to have the broker review it with you. If there is no broker involved and the contract is simply one purchased at the local office supply store designed to be legal in every state, it is definitely in the buyer's interest to consult with an attorney before signing.

TEACHING POINT: A word to the wise if you are buying a home to be built by a developer. These are commonly known as *house-lot packages* where the builder sells you the lot and then builds the house on it. These contracts are often very vague, sometimes not professionally written, and a buyer of such a property should always consult with an attorney prior to signing.

CONDOMINIUM DOCUMENTS

"Nobody reads the condominium documents." This is a bold statement, and of course technically is not true. First, there are people who do read them, the lawyers who draft them and a minority of those people who make condominium purchases. But it is safe to say that the vast majority of purchasers do not read these often massive documents, and that is a mistake.

Condominium documents are the legal blueprint of the building. The United States operates, in its purest form, on the basis of the Declaration of Independence, the Constitution, and the Bill of Rights. The condominium documents are the equivalent of those hallowed documents for the condominium owners, and they are not very difficult to understand. Condominium documents are generally divided into three parts, the declaration, the articles of incorporation, and the rules and regulations. Cooperative documents will differ slightly in content because the declaration is different...

..., ... the developer. Obviously this doesn't happen in real life, but rather, the condominium documents are recorded in the courthouse by the developer's attorneys. Recording provides the world with "legal knowledge" as to a specific item. In this case, the nature of the developers project.

The declaration will also identify the name of the condominium, the developer, and its principal officers. Don't be surprised if the developer in the declaration is not the same as the developer touted in the sales brochures. Sometimes, a developer will create a shell corporation for the purposes of liability protection. The shell corporation is the "official developer," while the more famous (and funded) counterpart is left out. This legal maneuver usually doesn't work, but it is often an expensive process to "pierce the corporate veil" to get to the real monied corporation or *deep pockets.*

At the end of the day, legitimate developers will stand behind their projects and not defend litigation on the basis of their phantom corporations. But if the declaration reveals a different corporate entity, it should raise a red flag to at least question the developer's representative on this issue. This goes back to our earlier discussion on researching a project prior to making a purchase.

The declaration has more relevance when purchasing directly from a developer than in a resale situation where the building is up and running with an association at the helm.

Articles of Incorporation

The second part of the condominium documents are *articles of incorporation.* This is really the meat and potatoes of the condominium documents. This portion will tell you your rights as a unit owner in the association. It deals with most issues from the rights and duties of the association board of directors, to whether a property owner is allowed to have pets. While it is often a very wordy document, the articles generally contain less "legalese" than one may imagine and it is not complicated to understand. Key issues to look for besides pet restrictions include rental policy, vehicle parking rights, limited common elements, leasehold obligations, and storage facilities.

Leasing Your Unit. The articles of incorporation will spell out whether the buyer can lease the unit and for what period of time. Examples range from not allowing a new purchaser to rent his or her unit for the first year or two to only allowing one rental per year irrespective of the length of time of that rental. There are all sorts of variations.

Vehicle Parking Rights. Parking rights are usually assigned, which means that the association tells you which parking space or spaces you are entitled to use. You may have the "right" to have one or more parking spaces, but not the right to choose which ones. However, with some condominiums parking spaces are *deeded*. This means you actually own your parking space along with your unit. This is different than merely having the right to have a space in the garage. Deeded parking is rare and usually comes with a premium price, especially if it is in a favored location of the parking area.

TEACHING POINT: The developer generally assigns spaces based on the cost of your unit. The more expensive the unit, the better the location of the parking space. For example, a choice spot may be one which is closest to the entrance to the lobby or main elevators, or where there are no stairs involved to get to your parking space. However, you can often negotiate your parking space location as part of your purchase, irrespective of the cost of your unit. Most developer representatives will dismiss this attempt by stating that "parking spaces have not been assigned yet." Be persistent, insist that your space be x number of feet from the lobby entrance. If you are getting two parking spaces and they are in tandem (one behind the other), try to negotiate side-by-side spaces. They are more convenient. Make sure to specify what you negotiate in writing as part of the contract.

Limited Common Elements. You will recall that common elements are those portions of the property such as the hallways, elevators, and amenities that are owned in common by all the residents. A *limited common element* is a portion of the property that is owned in common by all the residents

g   ,   association must repair it from association funds as opposed to the inside of your unit, which is your responsibility. In addition, the association can mandate what decorations may be put on your terrace. For example, a light fixture may not be allowed on your terrace because limited common elements are within the jurisdiction of the association.

If your parking space is not deeded, it is a limited common element as well. It is property owned in common but under the assigned owner's exclusive control.

TEACHING POINT: Certain condominiums, especially in oceanfront property, offer cabanas. These are small studio units situated by the pool or beach where owners can relax, perhaps shower, or entertain their friends while at the beach. If the cabanas are deeded, then they are real property to do with as the owner wishes so long as it is not prohibited by condominium rules and regulations. For example, many condominium documents provide that cabanas must first be offered to other unit owners and if no unit owner wants to purchase it, then it may be sold to anyone regardless of whether or not they own property in the building. This does not prevent the owner from selling an apartment separately from his or her cabana.

However, if the cabana is a limited common element, then the association may prevent the unit owner from selling his apartment until he transfers or assigns his rights to the cabana to another party, which must almost always be another unit owner. If nobody wants the cabana, the owners may be prevented from selling the unit unless they can find a buyer who will also buy the cabana. There have been a number of cases where associations have prevented sales of units because the purchaser did not buy the rights to the cabana, where the cabana was a limited common element.

TEACHING POINT: When purchasing additional parking, storage spaces, and cabanas, it is important to determine whether you are receiving deeded property or whether it is a limited common element. How can you find out? Simple—the condominium documents contain all the information on common and limited common elements of the building.

Leasehold Obligations. Leasehold obligations are an important factor to know about because they translate into ownership rights and money. With the advent of such newer type projects as hotel-condominiums or condominiums that contain both residential condominiums and hotel-condominiums in one building, it is important to understand who owns what portions of the project.

In one particular project, many owners were surprised to learn that they did not own their amenities and they were required to valet park their cars rather than have a choice to either park them themselves or use the valet service. While they had the right to have one car space in the garage, they did not have the right to a specific space and they could not park their own vehicles. In addition, the amenities, including the tennis courts, swimming pools, and gymnasium, were owned by the hotel contractor who operated the hotel portion of the project. Thus, if the hotel ran an event such as a pool party for its guests, it could theoretically and legally preclude unit owners from using the pool. Owners were even more surprised to learn that this was all spelled out clearly in their condominium documents.

Crimes and Punishments. Association documents may contain other important information as well. For example, what happens if you disobey a rule of the association? Can the association punish you? In many cases, the answer is yes. Condominium documents often provide the board the power to fine you for disobeying the association rules provided you are given certain rights to appeal the fine. This is usually done through an association judicial committee formed by the board and consisting of other unit owners. The documents spell out the procedures and monetary limitations for fining a unit owner.

Architectural Drawings. Most condominium documents also contain architectural drawings of the individual units and the building itself. This is to define common area elements, limited common area elements, and private property. It is important because it determines what the

Rules and Regulations

The third portion of the condominium documents is usually the *rules and regulations*. These are the implementation of day-to-day activities in the units. Items such as where and how pets may be transported through the building, the swimming pool hours, use of the elevators and general decorum in the common element areas may be found here.

It is important to know and understand the rules of the association before making the purchase. For example, if the condominium prohibits noise after 10:00 P.M. and you are a big party person, this building may not be for you if you are planning to occupy the unit and conduct a late-night social life. Many people who don't read the rules often find themselves in a constant battle with the association, and ultimately give up and sell their units.

TEACHING POINT: Most buildings have reasonable rules that are not difficult to obey. Although the condominium documents may look daunting and most people just take them and put them in a storage closet, it is worth the effort to sift through them before going ahead with the final purchase.

Reviewing the Association Budget

Some states require that the last budget of the association also be given to the potential purchaser. This gives the buyer the opportunity to study how effectively the association spends the money it takes in. If you are not a numbers person, this will not help you very much, but you may wish to show it to your accountant, or to someone who does appreciate numbers. Thus far, there is nothing daunting about any of the process in purchasing a condominium style investment. It does, however, require the purchasers to spend some time studying the documentation.

THE CLOSING PROCESS

The next phase of the purchase is the closing. We'll assume that any financing arrangements (which are discussed in Chapter 8) have been completed and you are ready to proceed with the closing of the property. The key issues in the closing process involve what is known as *marketable title,* approval by the condominium association (if necessary), and determination of closing costs.

In Chapter 6, we discussed the association approval process. Before discussing title issues and closing costs, let's look at whether an attorney is necessary at the closing.

Using an Attorney

When purchasing from a developer, you may or may not wish to employ an attorney if you are satisfied with the terms of the purchase. However, we always suggest that an attorney be present just to make sure that your rights are protected. There may not be much to negotiate at the closing, but should there be a problem, the developer generally has his or her attorney close the purchase and you should have one present as well. In case of a dispute, you will be well served to have a professional at your side.

I recall one of our first closings. We had purchased a condominium and prior to the closing had our walk-through. The unit had been ransacked. The refrigerator was gone, the stove was destroyed, the walls were a mess, and a wall mirror that came with the apartment was completely shattered. At the closing, the developer insisted we close and that the damage would be repaired. The developer's attorneys threatened to default us if we didn't close. Fortunately, we employed our own lawyer (since I didn't wish to represent us at our own transaction). He forced the developer to fix the damages first by pointing out that these damages were not mere construction defects but vandalism, and that the developer had breached its duty to adequately protect the unit. We prevailed and the closing was postponed until the unit was repaired. At that point, my wife and I were so upset that I doubt we would have been objective enough to make that cogent argument, or that the attorneys for the developer would have listened to us.

In the case of a resale, the buyer's side does most of the work to prepare for closing. The inspections, title search, insurance, and preparation of the closing statement are usually handled by the buyer's side. The seller's obligation is to provide proof of good title and that's pretty much it, other than to make sure that he or she is getting the right amount of money after closing expenses. Therefore, the buyer should employ an attorney or [1]

...... insurance policy, which is simply an insurance policy that the title to the property is marketable. Simply put, the title insurance company insures that the seller owns and can transfer the property free of any claims to that property by others. It is up to the buyer to check and update the seller's title to see that it is good or marketable.

We recently had a situation where a condominium was being sold for cash. There were no problems and both parties were being represented by the same title company. As we proceeded toward closing, the buyer's broker called to tell us that his client didn't want to purchase title insurance. The buyer felt that the building was brand new from the developer and the seller (our client) only owned the unit for a couple of weeks before "flipping" it to her. We were a bit taken aback. In our 25 years of experience, no buyer ever refused to purchase title insurance. The buyer's broker was equally dumbfounded. "What do I tell her; can she refuse to buy title insurance?" The answer is yes, since this was to be a cash deal. The banks will require title insurance as a condition of the mortgage, but where it is a cash deal, there is no such requirement. Therefore, the buyer in this situation is not required to purchase title insurance.

Of course, it is unwise to save money on title insurance, for a variety of reasons. First, buying from a developer is no absolute guarantee that the developer had good title. It merely indicates that the title insurance company is satisfied that it could defend any claims against the developer. That insurance policy is between the seller and the title insurance company. It won't extend to the new buyer. If there is ever a claim against the developer's title, the insurance company is under no obligation to defend the new buyer.

Second, it is possible that the seller could have committed or *encumbered* the property to another and therefore clouded the title. When you have title insurance, the insurance company will act as a guarantee for the title to the property. Think of it this way, you would not drive a car (and in many states you can't) without car insurance. Most people have medical insurance and life insurance. Why wouldn't you want title insurance on your property?

The third reason for purchasing title insurance is that when you sell your property, you, as the seller, will now have to present evidence of good title. If you don't have a current title policy, it will be more expensive for you to provide proof of good title when you sell.

When title to a property is successfully conveyed, the instrument or document that indicates this is called the *deed*. There are two types of deeds you need to be familiar with, the general warranty deed and the statutory warranty deed. Historically, the type of deed you received made a difference because it determined against whom you would have to defend the land. Often this was achieved by sending your army to fight the claimant. With a *general warranty deed,* theoretically, you the seller would be required to defend against anyone who lays claim against the title. With a *special warranty deed,* you would be required to defend only against direct descendants (previous title holders) to the property. Today, there is little practical difference between a special and a general warranty deed, and either is acceptable, depending on the custom of the area.

CAUTION: A *quit-claim deed* is a different type of deed. This deed guarantees nothing. It merely states that the holder of the deed grants whatever *rights, title, and interest* he has in the property to the receiving party. If the grantor of the deed holds no rights, title, or interest in the property, or his or her rights are defective, than that is simply what he or she conveys. Except for interfamily transfers to add children or conveyances of that nature, quit-claim deeds are a red flag that there might be some problem with the title of a property.

If a title company is employed, there is no conflict of interest if the company represents both the buyer and the seller. The title company assigns the expenses in accordance with the terms of the contract.

The Closing Statement

The closing statement, also known as the HUD 1 or simply HUD for Housing and Urban Development Form, is the form used to calculate and illustrate the closing costs. You will notice that the HUD form has two columns, one for the buyer's expenses and one for the seller's. At the bottom of the first page, the form tells how much the seller receives and how much the buyer pays. The bottom of the second page provides the detailed settlement charges to the buyer and the seller. The rest of the form merely lists the various expenses and how they were prorated. If you h~~~~ ~~~~~~~~~ ~

~~ ~~ ~~~~~~ ~~~~ ~~~~ property 101.

The more challenging portion of the closing statement is the recording and transfer charges, which are more commonly known as *stamps*. These charges can really add up. Basically, stamps are the fees charged by the state and local governments for allowing you to perform the real estate transaction. It is a transaction tax on each type of transaction that needs to be recorded, and there are various types. For example, there are recording fees for the deed and mortgages. If the seller has a mortgage that is being paid off at the closing, that is recorded as well. Each state has its own system of charging stamps, but usually it is based on a percentage of the purchase price of the property.

TEACHING POINT: You don't have to understand each and every charge. The broker, attorney, or closing agent can explain them to you. What you need to be aware of is whether the proration is correct and in keeping with the terms of the contract.

Calculating Prorations

How prorations are calculated is defined in the contract, and it is generally taken as of the date of the closing unless the contract stipulates some other formula. Thus, if you close on March 18, if you are the buyer, your ownership is calculated as of that date, and all costs from that day forth are attributed to you; the seller pays for everything up to that date. Mistakes in the closing statement can occur either in the math or in reading the terms of the contract. It is up to both the seller and the buyer to check the figures. Mistakes in HUD statements are not very common but they do occur, and they are often a result of either mathematical error or misreading of the contract and, thus, attributing costs to the wrong parties.

Review the Statement in Advance

As indicated in a recent teaching point, the closing table is not the time to take out your calculator and copy of your contract and start doing math. As the buyer (or the seller, for that matter), you will want to see your figures in advance. You should have your closing statement at least three days before the closing, which should give you plenty of time to review it for accuracy. However, this may or may not occur, depending on a number of factors.

Where there is a mortgage involved, the bank has to provide its figures to the closing agent before the final calculations can be made. In a busy real estate market, banks may not look at your file until one or two days prior to the closing. This often creates a great deal of stress on everyone, but especially buyers, who need to know what their closing costs are going to be.

Another factor in busy real estate areas are closing agents who don't get to the file until a day before the closing. To avoid this situation, start calling the bank or the closing agent about two weeks before the scheduled date of the closing. Be persistent, and your file should move to the top of the list. Some states require that the broker and bank provide good-faith estimates of closing costs. However, these estimates are just that, good faith. Final costs may differ considerably from the good-faith estimates. So keep pestering for that closing statement; it will take a great deal of stress out of the transaction.

If all else fails, you may cite federal law. The Real Estate Settlement Procedures Act (RESPA) applies to mortgage brokers and lenders. Of particular note is that under RESPA, lending institutions are required to provide you with a HUD one business day before closing. Federal law in this regard overrides any specific portion of the real estate contract or loan agreement. We take a more detailed look at RESPA in the next chapter on mortgages.

TEACHING POINT: Review the HUD before you walk into the settlement room for your closing.

In the next two chapters, we will discuss financing and mortgages, which will fill in some of the gaps of this chapter. In Chapter 8, we will also continue with our discussion of closings and what to expect at the closing table.

CHAPTER 8

You have found the ideal property. You must have it. Unfortunately, you don't have $500,000 in spare cash to make the purchase. In fact, it might not even be a good idea to use it even if you did. What is the alternative? Simple: Borrow the money from a bank or other lending institution. Actually, the word *simple* may not be the proper term. Borrowing money can be a more complex transaction than the purchase of the property itself, and making the right choices when seeking a loan may make the difference in whether your real estate purchase will be a wise one or not.

The basic reaction of a buyer who is going to finance the purchase of a property is to go see his or her local banker, the friendly person at the local branch who gave you the toaster when you opened your checking account. After all, you know this person, your money is in his or her bank, and you think your bank will give you the best deal. There is nothing particularly wrong with this philosophy, as far as it goes. That is the same reaction that my wife and I have when we purchase a property. But there are two things that you need to understand. The first is that there are many types of lending institutions with different rates who may be willing to lend you money, and second, your friendly banker will help you in the initial stages of the loan but thereafter has little to say about it.

Most people should and do consider their local bank to be a safer and friendlier environment where they will get better terms. However, you may not be better off dealing with your local bank for getting the best loan rate and terms, or *product,* as the loan is often referred to in the industry. In this chapter, we will explore the loan process, some of the products that are being offered, and the various types of institutions and professionals available to help you secure a loan. We will start our discussion with the bank.

BANK LOANS

Banks are the main source of lending, and that is their essential function. They are in business to use your money to make money. They lend money at interest, and that interest represents their profit. It is all about investing. You are investing in real estate by buying property, and they are investing in that same purchase by lending you the money at interest. Our key rule, business is business, still applies. The bank is looking to get the most money it can by loaning you money while you should be trying to get the best deal; to wit, the best rate and terms from the bank.

For example, we own a condominium that we believe has reached the point where we should now sell it. However, the terms we secured with the bank are so favorable that we can well afford to hold on to it until we get the price we want. We are not pressured to accept lower offers because of the favorable rate and terms. Further, had we decided to rent the property, the low monthly payments would mean a greater net return on our rental income.

A positive point worth noting is that there are lots of products available today, especially with the new companies appearing on the Internet. With an increase in the supply of mortgage money, the banks have to compete and therefore offer more interesting and favorable terms in order to secure your business. First, let us look at the way the loan process operates and then we'll explore the differences between the various institutions who are vying for your business.

Processing the Loan

The loan process is generally the same no matter what type of lending institution you employ. The first stage of the process is to take your loan application. This is a standard form used by all lenders wherein your basic financial information is requested. You should be prepared to provide the sources and amounts of your income, as well as your liabilities such as credit card debt and other monthly expenses. In some cases, your friendly banker will be able to *prequalify* you. He or she will type your information and a few seconds later will proudly exclaim that you are *approved*. Unfortunately, that is a very optimistic use of the term. What the banker should proudly exclaim is that you are "tentatively approved subject to the entire lending

amount of your existing obligations, as opposed to your income. It may require proof of income, such as two or three years of tax returns and pay slips from your employer. It will factor in your credit score (which we will discuss in more detail shortly) and the real estate investment itself.

Not all banks loan on every property. Some banks will not loan on hotel-condominiums, while others won't loan on cooperatives. The bank will usually require an appraisal of the property to ascertain if the value of the property can be recovered if you default on the loan. This is where the comparables that we discussed in the chapters on buying and selling become important in the loan process. When a property is sold at some outrageous amount of money not previously received by any other seller, the buyer may not be able to get financing because there is no evidence that the property can really command that price and the bank does not want to be the first to lend at the new amount. This usually occurs in a hot real estate market.

The bank will also consider how much money you put down as a deposit in the investment. Generally, the banks will look at 20 percent or more as being optimal. Although some banks will loan up to 100 percent or even more, most want to see some investment in the property on the part of the purchaser. In addition, where there is less than a 20 percent investment in the property by the buyer, the banks will require you to purchase mortgage insurance, which could be a costly added expense. The next section has more to say on down payments.

The bank will require certain documents from the condominium association, such as proof of building insurance. Some banks will also want to know what the ratio is of owners living in the building to tenants who are renting their apartments. As a rule of thumb, if the building is more than 40 percent rental property, banks may be hesitant to loan money on the property because they fear the owners have little incentive to adequately maintain the property. Many banks and lending institutions prefer to see a significant portion of resident owners.

Once the loan processor finishes his or her job, the package goes to the underwriter, who we sometimes dub *the undertaker* because he or she can unilaterally approve or disapprove a loan package. In fact, it is the job of the underwriter to review each loan package and he or she may approve, disapprove, or send the package back to the processor for more information. Underwriters are usually meticulous in their investigations because if they approve a bad loan, they are responsible for making the call. In other words, while they have almost absolute power over the approval or disapproval of the loan, if the loan is bad, they must face the wrath of the bank as well. It is only in the rarest of cases that an underwriter's decision is overruled, or the file transferred to another underwriter for further review where one underwriter disapproves the loan. A decision to challenge an underwriter is made at a level far higher than your friendly banker who took your loan application.

In some cases, the underwriter may approve a loan, but with a change of terms. This could be reflected in a higher rate, lower amount of money to be lent, or shorter period of time for the payoff.

Economic Issues

The economic ramifications of securing a loan are far reaching. When you attempt to secure a loan, lenders are going to evaluate three key pieces of information: your credit history, your down payment, and your tax returns.

Credit History. The first and major ramification involves the use of credit. In the United States, as in most capitalist societies, you need credit to obtain credit. Thus, you may have paid all of your bills your whole life on time and in cash, and you have zero debt. However, when it comes to securing a loan for a property, because you have no credit history, you will have trouble being approved. Thus, it is important to establish a credit history. This can be done by having a major credit card that you use and pay each month on time.

Other creditworthiness indicators are prompt payment of utility bills such as phone and, more importantly, electricity. Most companies will report credit problems when bills are late more than 30 days. Many credit card companies will advance you additional credit to avoid your being embarrassed at the venue where you are using the credit card. But it is crucial that you repay the overage as soon as the credit card company notifies you, or get an increase in the amount of your credit line on your card if the credit card company is willing to do so. Either way, you usually have a 30-day window to resolve the issue, but you need to follow the terms set out by your credit card issuer.

it to say that in terms of securing a mortgage, there is only one thing you need to be aware of. Your credit score will determine if you get a mortgage in the first place. If your score is high enough to qualify you for a mortgage, your score will be influential in determining your interest rate. A poorer score may still qualify you for a mortgage but at a higher interest rate. Therefore, it is incumbent upon you to make sure that your scores are the highest they can possibly be.

Your Down Payment. The bank or lending institution is going to ask for a lot of information that you may think is none of its business. You may be right, except that you may not have a choice if you want to get a loan. In most cases, the bank is concerned with the deposit. Although some institutions will lend at up to, and sometimes more than, 100 percent, most want to see a deposit or *down payment* of between 10 percent and 20 percent. Banks prefer to have you as a partner in the transaction with enough equity in the property so you will be encouraged to make your payments. They don't really want to front the entire loan for you.

The next question the lender will want to know is, where did that money come from? If you borrowed it from your grandmother, this could be a problem, because the lender wants *you* to have money. It doesn't care about your grandmother's finances unless her name is going to be on the loan. The other issue is that the government and the banks are concerned with money laundering, which is simply the legitimizing of unlawfully obtained funds through legitimate channels, such as the purchase of real estate. If it turns out that the condominium you have purchased was paid for with unlawfully obtained funds, the government could confiscate the property and the lender would be out its interest and its collateral. So it will often want to see at least three months of bank statements or other evidence to show that the funds were yours and how you acquired those funds. Thus, if all of sudden a sum equal to a 20 percent down payment were to appear in your account, the bank would want to know where those funds came from. If they came from Granny—or a particularly successful jewel heist—that might be a problem.

Many condominiums now require up to a 20 percent deposit prior to approving the sale, to ensure that the buyer can meet his or her financial obligations to the association once the property is acquired. This means the seller or the association will want to see a cash deposit in the broker's or attorney's escrow in accordance with the terms of the contract.

READ AND HEED: When purchasing a resale, deposit funds should be placed in *your* broker's or attorney's escrow account, not the buyer's. Rules for broker's escrow accounts are generally more stringent than those of attorneys in terms of when funds may be released. Never give the deposit directly to the seller. This is in case a dispute arises. You want those funds secure until the dispute is resolved. When purchasing from a developer, you won't have that option; however, most reputable developers contract with an escrow agent to hold the funds.

Your Tax Returns. Banks love tax returns, especially from those people who are self-employed. Tax returns can be a two-edged sword, and the banks know it. Let's suppose you have your own business and a portion of your business is done in cash, as opposed to checks or credit card receivables. The law requires that you declare cash as income, but you succumb to temptation and don't declare your cash income. In addition, you have a bunch of expenses that you pad nicely so that your tax return shows a lot less income than you actually receive. Moral and legal pronouncements aside, you are very happy with your tax returns. However, now you are in front of your banker, and he is asking for your income. You tell him that you earn plenty of money and don't have too many debts. "That's great," he replies, "Just show us your tax returns for the last three years and we'll be fine." Oops, now you have a problem. You need to present yourself as having a strong financial position, and your tax returns will not support it. In fact, according to your tax returns, you have a rather weak financial picture.

There is an old lawyer's saying, "Never steal from your client's escrow and don't mess with the IRS." I believe in that saying. I believe that everyone should take advantage of lawful deductions that the government provides in the tax code. However, at the end of the day, you can outsmart yourself by being too creative with your taxes in many ways—including

and the collateral, the property itself.

Alternatives to Bank Loans

As already stated, the loan process is basically the same no matter what type of institution you use. It is always a good policy to see your bank first and get its best deal. Then you may wish to consult either a mortgage broker or mortgage banker. A *mortgage broker* is simply an agent who shops for different loans and submits them on your behalf. A *mortgage banker* represents an institution that can actually loan you the money. A mortgage banker is in the business solely to lend money and does not have any of the other banking services you get with your local branch. It is not a bank per se but rather a money-lending company. Both mortgage bankers and mortgage brokers are regulated by applicable federal and state regulations and must make certain disclosures to you, which we will discuss later in this chapter.

TEACHING POINT: While shopping for the best rates is important, some care should be exercised in doing so. Once you know that your credit is good and the property of your choice is one that lenders are willing to lend on, you are pretty much in the driver's seat in terms of shopping your loan. The trick is not to let each broker or banker take your credit application, because each time your credit is run, it lowers your credit score slightly. Most will want to take your credit application, or app, first. Resist the temptation to give this information. Find out what loan packages the lending institution is offering first. Unless the loan representative offers you a package with rates and terms that you really want to qualify for, don't fill out an application.

Types of Mortgages

When shopping for a loan, you will be confronted and possibly confounded by the myriad of loan packages available on the market. It is impossible to deal with all of them, but we will give you the basics so you can figure them out more easily.

Fixed-Rate Mortgages

The basic type of loan is generally called a fixed-rate 30-year loan. This, as the title implies, is a loan for a fixed interest rate that will be paid off completely after paying principal and interest for 30 years. The interest, of course, is the profit to the bank.

Presumably, you will sell the property before the 30-year term is up. When that happens, the lender calculates how much interest you have paid and how much principal is left due and owing. The lender will deduct it's debt from the sales price. Some banks charge what is known as a *prepayment penalty*. This means that if you pay off the loan prior to its expiration, the lender gets to charge you extra penalties. If you can at all help it, don't take a loan with a prepayment penalty. It's just gravy for the lender. We'll discuss prepayment penalties in more detail below.

Fixed-rate 30-year loans are not the only kind of loans banks offer. For example, the bank may offer you a fixed-rate 20- or 15-year loan, or even a fixed-rate 10-year loan. The difference is that over the course of 10 or 15 years you pay less interest than over 30 years. However, because you are paying the principal back in a shorter period of time, your monthly payments are going to be higher. So it really is a tradeoff. Do you want to pay less interest and pay off your mortgage in a shorter period, or do you want to pay lower monthly payments for a longer period? As we shall see shortly, it is going to depend on a variety of factors.

Another variation to this scenario is a fixed-rate interest-only loan. In this case, you are paying a fixed interest rate over the period of the loan, but you are not paying any principal off. Each month you are paying only the interest. At the expiration of the loan, you will still owe the lender the entire principal amount of the loan. What is the advantage of this type of loan? The monthly payments will be even lower, because now there is no money going towards principal but, rather, you are just paying the interest.

Adjustable Rate Mortgages

The next type of loan available is called the adjustable rate mortgage, or the A.R.M. The A.R.M. has many variations and unless you really under-

your rate is based will not go up, or better yet, will go down. If it goes up, there is usually a cap on how high your interest rate will be. If there is no cap, pass on that particular type of loan.

There are some interesting little traps with regard to an A.R.M. One such trap is called *negative amortization*. The cap on the increase of your loan based on a rise in the U.S. Treasury Securities index does not cover increases in the interest rate; it only caps the overall monthly payment. Negative amortization occurs if the payment cap is not enough to cover the increase in the interest rate. In this case, the amount of your debt is increased by the shortfall of the interest payment not covered by the monthly payment cap. Therefore, your debt will be increasing rather than decreasing as you continue to make payments.

NAVIGATING THE TERMINOLOGY

There are some terms you should be familiar with as you navigate the mortgage process. These terms are buydowns, points, prepayment penalties, and breakeven.

Buydowns

The *buydown* is simply a method by which you can lower your interest rate with the lending institution. Very simply stated, you, the borrower, pay the lending institution a sum of money in advance. In turn, the lending institution lowers the rate of the mortgage. In the consumer handbook that must be given to you by the lending institution, the buydown is defined as the seller making the buydown payment. That's nice in theory, but in the real world, you the borrower will negotiate and pay the buydown and the seller will rarely be involved unless he or she is helping you with the financing per your contract with that seller. Sometimes, the bank will allow you to subsidize the buydown. This means that your monthly payments will be based on a lower monthly rate but the subsidy will be tacked on to the principal amount of the loan and so in the long run, you are still paying for the buydown.

Points

Another concept you need to understand is *points*. One point equals 1 percent of the amount of principal of your mortgage. Points are additional fees that the bank charges for costs associated with the loan. Banks have all sorts of fees. For example, if you purchase a condominium in a building with over a certain amount of units, there is a fee; or if the loan is for over a certain amount of money, it is considered a jumbo loan, and there is a fee for that. The amount of points reflect those fees. There are other fees as well, and these can be hefty.

Prepayment Penalties

If at all possible, you should avoid *prepayment penalties*. We have already established that mortgages are a source of income for the lender. The lender is in the business to make money by lending you money. The longer you pay, the more interest the lender makes on its loan. On one hand, it is not in the interest of the lender or *mortgagor* to have you pay back the loan too fast. On the other hand, it is certainly to the borrower's or *mortgagee's* advantage to pay the loan back as quickly as possible. Thus, if you take out a 30-year fixed-rate mortgage and sell your property in five years, the lender stands to lose 25 years' worth of interest. That is a lot of money.

To help rectify the situation, and to discourage early payoffs, the lenders often charge what is known as a *prepayment penalty*. This penalty is a sum of money charged to the borrower as a punishment for early repayment of the debt. Our advice is, if there is a prepayment penalty, don't take the loan.

Some prepayment penalties are disguised, and you have to be careful. For example, your banker or mortgage broker may say there is no prepayment penalty on the loan. But upon closer inspection, you find that in fact there is a prepayment penalty for the first few years of the loan (let's say three years as an example), and then it goes away after the third year, or there is a declining penalty, depending on how long you keep the loan.

Even if you believe you will keep the property for more than three years, for example, you may still wish to avoid a prepayment penalty. Let us suppose that in the second year of the loan, interest rates drop and you wish to refinance your loan at a better rate. You certainly would not want any prepayment penalties to apply. Most prepayment penalty cl

...ly ... how long you plan to keep your property. For example, if you estimate that you are going to hold your property for ten years before selling, you can calculate the amount of money you spend in buydowns and points and determine when the *breakeven* is, as opposed to the amount of money you will save over the ten-year period of time in lower monthly payments. If you pay back the points or buydowns in three years and the next seven years represent a substantial savings in terms of the lower rates, than it pays to do the buydown. If the breakeven point is in five years and you plan to keep the property for only three years, then you haven't yet taken advantage of any buydown savings and you should not buy down the rate.

The same analysis would apply to a prepayment penalty. If the mortgage carries a prepayment penalty for the first five years of the loan and you estimate you will be keeping the property for seven years, it may not be so critical to reject the loan based on the prepayment penalty clause, if the other terms are very favorable. But it is still a gamble. We have a client who purchased a property that he estimated he would retain for five to seven years. His mortgage has a three-year prepayment penalty. The investment was very successful and appreciated more quickly than anticipated. However, with his prepayment penalty, it still didn't make sense for him to sell and pay off the loan, so he has elected to wait another year until the penalty expires.

FEES AND COMMISSIONS

Again, we stress the point that mortgages are business and there are a number of players involved, depending on how you go about getting your mortgage. For example, suppose that you employ a mortgage broker to secure the best possible mortgage for you. That mortgage broker is paid a commission, which comes out of your closing costs with the bank. Sometimes, the broker will reduce the commission and/or fees to help you out. Does that mean the broker is a great person? Maybe, but not all the time.

Mortgage brokers sometimes get paid on the back end of the mortgage by the lending institutions, as well as the front end in fees by you the borrower, but it is all charged to you one way or another. Unfortunately, unless you examine in great detail the portion of the closing statement relating to the mortgage, this will not be evident. There is no specific category called "back end fees to mortgage broker." These are hidden fees often placed in such categories as miscellaneous settlement charges such as "yield spread."

This is how it generally works. If you qualify for a lower rate with the lender than what the broker actually sells you, the broker may qualify for a *yield spread* payable to the broker. In other words, the mortgage broker gets a bonus on top of the commission for selling you a more expensive product than you could have gotten (which translates into more profit for the bank), and you get to pay for that bonus as well. New legislation in some states requires full disclosure of yield spreads to the buyer. However, legislation has allowed up to 10 percent of the mortgage amount as payment to the mortgage bank or broker.

TEACHING POINT: These fees are negotiable as well. They are negotiable if you know the right questions to ask. It's your money, and you have every right to question how much you are paying for this loan and to whom. Your mortgage broker may be making more money on the back end than the front, and the bank is charging you for all of this directly or indirectly. The only way to know how much the mortgage broker is getting is to directly ask the broker and demand full disclosure and explanations.

So how do you deal with all of this information on mortgages and loans? By taking the time to carefully examine your loan agreement and to make sure that the bank, the closing agent, and the seller (especially if you are dealing with a developer) provide you with all the information well in advance of the loan or else postpone the closing until you have all the information. The best way to try to bring it all together for you is with a case study.

STICKER SHOCK AT THE CLOSING

Let me give you an example of what happened to my wife and I on a recent purchase. We discussed this example in a different context in the

mated closing costs, which included an estimate of the costs charged by the developer. Both our bank and the developer's mortgage company gave similar estimates as to closing costs, and we accepted those as fact. We didn't demand to see the actual closing statement until the day of the closing. To our surprise, the costs were about $21,000 over everyone's projections.

We were in shock, but what could we do? The costs were lawful, if you carefully and skillfully represented a very broad interpretation of the terms of the contract with the developer. Did the bank do anything wrong? Clearly not—the terms of the loan were what we had negotiated with the bank. It apportioned costs in terms of the information provided to them by the developer as well as our agreement with the bank. As it turns out, the lending institutions did not understand the developer's contract and underestimated what we were obligated to pay in terms of closing costs.

Everyone who bought in that project had to pay just as we did. What did we do wrong? We didn't get the final closing statement until we walked into the closing room. Remember, the closing table is not the place to negotiate. Even our own attorneys were stunned, but unless we walked away from the deal and risked losing our substantial deposit, we were forced to close, just like the other 300-odd stunned purchasers. For us, as professionals, it was an amateurish mistake based on overconfidence. So let's start from the beginning of the transaction and to the fateful and expensive day at our closing and hopefully, you won't make the same mistake we did.

Reviewing the Details

In south Florida, most developers have in their contracts a clause that states that the buyer will pay 1.5 to 1.7 percent of the sales price of the property to defray the costs of the closing. The sales agent always tries to explain that this is cheaper for everyone because the developer gets better bulk rates and there are less administrative costs involved.

In the beginning, we used to fight this fee, but most developers are firm and won't negotiate this point. In this case, we just considered it an additional fee and concentrated on getting the best price for the unit we could, factoring in the 1.7 percent charge as best we could. This was our first mistake. At that point, early in the negotiation, we should have demanded an in-depth analysis of what the 1.7 percent covered. We could have gotten this from our attorneys or from the developer. In Florida, you have a 14-day rescission period when you buy a condominium from a developer, which means you have two weeks to back out of the deal. This would have been more than enough time to figure it out. My wife has a master's degree in business, and I'm a lawyer. Between the two of us, we could have figured it out ourselves, but we didn't bother.

We next proceeded to negotiate our loan. Since a developer's contract is not subject to our being able to secure financing, we did this within the 14 days of rescission. My wife negotiated a very favorable loan agreement with the bank as well as with the developer's lending institution, and both entities gave us our disclosure forms. This is a very important aspect of the loan process, and we need to digress a bit to discuss it in some detail.

Analyzing the Disclosure Forms

A loan generally takes about 30 to 60 days average to process, and unless you plan to get a degree in finance, how do you get all the knowledge you need to analyze your loan? Certainly not by reading one chapter in a book. Actually, federal law requires that the banks give you certain disclosures. In fact, the law requires that you be provided with almost every aspect of the bank's transaction with you. You will be given so much information, in such detail, that most of it won't make any sense. Most borrowers will just confirm the interest rate and forget the rest. This can cost you money. My bank had some 31 different estimated charges representing thousands of dollars, and some were unintelligible. This included its estimation of what would and would not be covered by the 1.7 percent developer's fee. These various charges were incorporated in what is referred to as a *good-faith settlement statement.*

The important point to remember with a good-faith settlement statement is, as the title implies, the bank or other lending institution is only estimating your costs. It is not bound by the estimate. Historically, we have found that these estimates are more or less accurate, although recently, our own bank has been coming in with much higher estimates, until we made our recent purchase. Our reliance on the good-faith estimate cost us a great deal of money. The question is, if the bank or lending i............ .

you have received a satisfactory answer. The trick is not to know everything there is to know about a subject, in this case, mortgages, but rather, know what questions to ask and when to ask them.

In our case, when we reviewed our contract, we knew that the 1.7 percent covered some closing costs, but we didn't bother to ask the right questions, and neither did the banks. In the past it was never a problem, so we were careless. You can rest assured that in the future, if we are faced with a developer fee that alleges to cover a certain category of costs, we will have all details and interpretations prior to signing the contract.

You probably will not encounter this type of fee unless you are purchasing directly from a developer. However, you will literally receive a mountain of disclosures from your lending institution, some of which are nonsense and some of which are very important.

The most important disclosure you will receive is a form that tells you the amount of the loan, the rate of interest being charged, the cost of the loan in dollars and how much you will have paid in total if you keep the loan for the duration of the mortgage. That form will also tell you if there are any prepayment penalties. It will give you your monthly payment amount or amounts, depending on what type of loan you negotiate.

If any information on the form does not agree with the terms and conditions of the loan you thought you were getting, you need to discuss it with your banker or mortgage broker. We will return to the forms and disclosures toward that end of the chapter, but now that you are familiar with the basics of the mortgage process, we need to discuss some of the legal and economic ramifications of securing a mortgage. First, we will discuss the legal aspects.

A MORTGAGE IS A LEGAL OBLIGATION

The mortgage process involves your borrowing money from a lending institution by securing your property as collateral for the loan. When you borrow money, you sign a mortgage and a note. The mortgage reflects the terms of the loan and the note is the evidence by which you place your property as collateral for the loan. In other words, as we said at the onset of this discussion, so long as you pay you stay—that is, you get to keep your property.

If you fail to make timely payments, the lending institution will take your property in a procedure known as a *foreclosure*. This is a legal process wherein the lending institution has the right to take your property and sell it to recoup its money. There are few defenses to a foreclosure action. The most common is that the bank failed to follow proper foreclosure procedures. For example, it failed to provide you with the legally required notices prior to or during the filing of the foreclosure action, the legal process to retake your property. Another is if the lending institution engaged in some sort of fraudulent activity regarding your loan. In either case, you may be able to stall the foreclosure, but you borrowed money and eventually you are going to have to pay it back.

A foreclosure will go on your credit history and can be devastating if you wish to secure new financing. It is therefore crucial that you understand the terms of your loan and are able to make the payments. Contrary to popular belief, lending institutions are not anxious to foreclose, they make their money on the fees and interest when they loan you the money. In many cases, when a lending institution takes your property in a foreclosure action and sells it, it may not recoup the full amount of the loan and you may still be liable for the difference. If you encounter problems with the repayment of the loan, it may be best to consult with your banker or an attorney before you fall too far behind. Some lending institutions will work with you to avoid foreclosure.

TOO GOOD TO BE TRUE?

There are lots of systems being touted that involve no-money-down purchases. We haven't explored each and every one of them, nor are we prepared to comment on these "get-rich-quick" systems where you literally buy property without cash. Many of these systems do involve distressed properties or distressed sellers who are anxious to cooperate in any scheme just to get out of their commitment. However, in most normal situations, a seller will want to see a deposit, and so will the bank.

~   —

~

.... a copy of the contract and needs to see it. Don't panic. Lending institutions are big bureaucracies, and their documents get lost in processing. Just fax a copy of the sales contract and that should solve the problem.

A few days later, you get another call from the loan processor. Now they need a copy of the condominium's insurance policy. Call the building manager and make sure he or she faxes to the number provided by the lender. Don't even bother to suggest that the lender call the manager unless the caller actually volunteers to do so—and even then, check with the manager to make sure it has been done.

READ AND HEED: About two weeks prior to the closing, start annoy-
     ing the lender. Remind the lender of the closing date, check the
     status of the loan package, and get frequent updates. Remember
     that regardless of whether or not it is the bank's fault, you are
     responsible for closing on the date assigned on the contract, and it
     is your responsibility to see that you are prepared to close on that
     date.

At the closing, you will be seated with the seller, or the seller's representative. This could be either an attorney or a closing agent, usually from a title company. That person will have the loan documents from the lending institution. In most cases, closing involves a massive amount of paperwork. The attorney or closing agent will not be representing you, but rather, he or she will be either representing the seller or the lender or both, even though they have your loan documents.

As we said earlier, it is only on rare occasions that the lender's representative or the mortgage broker actually goes to the closing. Again, this is not the time to be looking at the closing statement for the first time. All of this should be a formality. If it is not, you did it wrong. Most of the documents you will be given to sign are disclosures and waivers. You agree to pay the monthly payments on time, you agree that you were not coerced into taking the loan, and you understand that the lending institution may sell or transfer your loan to another company. That's correct—many lenders sell their loans to other companies. Don't worry, they have to do so at the same price and terms, and it won't make much of a difference to you either way, except where you send the check. Major banking institutions generally don't sell their loans, but they retain the right to do so.

The closing agent may ask you if you opted for automatic payments. Hopefully, you did. We recommend it. It is a cleaner system, and it is very important that you make your payments on time, both for this and future credit. Just be sure you always have enough funds in the bank to cover the payment. This way, there are no mistakes with mail, travel, coupons getting lost, and so on.

There is another issue that you should be aware of—that is, whose name the property will be in, and whose name will be on the mortgage.

Oddly enough, many banks and lending institutions will allow you to have the mortgage in your name alone but have the property in both yours and your spouse's name, or vice versa. You need to check with your bank or lending institution to be certain. However, if you change your mind after you close, the bank could charge you another recording fee, which could mean thousands of dollars in expenses, depending on the cost of the property. So be certain about whose name you wish to have the property in prior to closing.

THE BENEFIT OF FINANCING

It is interesting to mention at this point the true benefit of financing a purchase and the reason we all go through this tedious mortgage process. Let's look at the percentage profit when you sell a mortgaged property, as compared to selling a property owned free and clear.

Say you make a purchase of a condominium for $200,000. In case A, you invest 20 percent, $40,000, in down payment. You then obtain financing for the remaining 80 percent. After two years of living in the property you sell the property for $320,000. What percentage did you make on your investment? You owed the bank $160,000, which comes off the top of the sale proceeds. So you get $160,000 in cash at closing (we won't consider closing and other related costs in this example). Remember, all you invested of your own money into this purchase was $40,000, not $200,000. The $160,000 came from the bank. So take off your original investment of $40,000 and that leaves you a profit of $120,000

, your first deal, but not as good, and you tied up your own capital for two years.

CHAPTER 9

Living in Your Condominium, Co-op, or Townhouse

You've bought, financed, and closed your dream condominium. Now it is time to move in. What are some of the things you are going to have to deal with? There will be a difference when you are moving into a newly constructed building as opposed to one that is up and operating, so let's focus on the worst-case scenario—buying a newly constructed condominium. It really isn't so bad if you know what to expect.

There are going to be at least seven things you, as a new property owner, are going to have to face:

1. Moving into the property
2. Working with the building manager
3. Decorating your unit
4. Obtaining the proper insurance
5. Paying special assessments
6. Figuring out the rules
7. Dealing with your neighbors

In this chapter, we will deal with these and other related topics.

MOVING INTO THE PROPERTY

Let us suppose that you purchased directly from the developer, preconstruction, an apartment on the twentieth floor of a building that contains

you gratefully tell your landlord you are leaving, notify the moving company of your closing date, and get ready to rock and roll into your new
apartment. You are already in trouble.

Taking Possession

The first rule of moving into any type of real estate is, "It ain't yours 'til
it's yours." In other words, until you close, you can't take possession of the
apartment. In some resale situations, the seller and the buyer can arrange to
allow the buyer to move in before the closing, but it generally does not
happen, and it is a very bad idea. We'll get further into that in Chapter 10,
but for now, assume that until you close on your property, you won't be
moving in. Consequently, contacting your moving company, giving notice
to your landlord, and in general, making preparations to move into your
unit before you are certain that the closing will take place as scheduled
constitutes very poor planning.

Scheduling Deliveries and Contract Work

The next problem, in a new development, is that you and 350 other purchasers are going to be competing for elevator space to move furniture,
flooring materials, paint, and whatever else is necessary to make your property habitable. Unless you coordinate your move with the building's management, you may find that your movers or contractors are turned away
when they show up to deliver their items. You don't want this to happen.
The moving industry has a one-way mentality. It may be very efficient
getting goods from point A to point B and off-loading it. It is, however,
not prepared to handle situations where it has been prevented from making
its delivery and having to return and store the items again. This does not

only incur added expense for the recipient, but is a prescription for loss of goods. So the first thing you want to do is verify that you have access to the building's elevators on the day your items arrive.

The other thing you want to do is be on location on the date your delivery arrives. Don't leave it to the building's personnel or the delivery company to get things done. They won't. You need to be there. If you have to take a day off work, do it!

READ AND HEED: If the association rules state that there can be no deliveries on Saturday, or after 5:00 P.M., don't do it. It will just cause you needless aggravation to try and circumvent the rules, and the building manager will be justified in denying permission for the delivery people to off-load. Always schedule deliveries for as early as you can.

Years ago, while I was on active military duty, we moved to a condominium near the Air Force Base where I was stationed. The rules of the condominium stated that no move-ins could occur after 5:00 P.M. during the week, and none on weekends. The movers were delayed and arrived at 5:01 P.M. on a Friday. They were denied entry, and all of our possessions were stored (at our expense) for the weekend, including my uniforms. It was highly embarrassing to show up at work on Monday morning in my jeans and tee shirt. Fortunately, the boss had a sense of humor, and I was given a day's leave to sort out my affairs. Nevertheless, this incident illustrates the fact that associations can and often do strictly enforce the rules.

Is Your Unit Finished?

Another problem is the fact that in the mad rush to move in to the new condominium or co-op, purchasers have often neglected to "finish" the unit. In the previous example, there is still painting and flooring to take place. These are not easy tasks. Contractors must also be coordinated with the building management, and there are often delays involved.

TEACHING POINT: Don't take anything for granted. Assume that there will be delays at every stage, and plan accordingly. If everything goes on schedule, great, but if not, you, the purchaser are not caught off guard without a place to live or clothes on your back.

Is the Building Finished?

The next problem purchasers of new construction often encounter is the fact that in many states, when a building receives its temporary certificate

take quite awhile.

If any or all of this happens, do not be shocked. It should all work out in time. Treat it as part of the move-in experience rather than cause for complaint. There are growing pains for newly constructed buildings, usually at least six months to a year.

Have You Checked for Problems?

There is one item that you should take very seriously, and most purchasers do not. That is your walk-through. Prior to your closing, you should have been afforded the opportunity to see your unit and, along with a representative of the developer, check the unit for problems. This should be done very carefully, because it will be your last opportunity to get down in writing any discrepancies in the unit.

Check everything carefully, including all the appliances. Remember, after you close, these things are your problem. If the oven doesn't work, the developer may say, "Don't worry, it is under warranty, just call the company." Prior to closing, you are justified in telling the representative to get you a new appliance. The developer has to provide you with new appliances, and they have to be in working condition. However, if it is not noted in the *punch list*, after you close, you'll have to deal with the appliance company.

Real-Life Case in Point

At this point, you may be thinking that this is all fairly obvious. Let me assure you that it is not. As of this writing, my wife and I purchased a unit from the developer in a new condominium complex. There are about 200 very smart, mostly affluent people who are experiencing the very examples just noted, and they are not happy. My wife and I are also experiencing it, but as the old saying goes, "Forewarned is forearmed." We haven't sold our old residence yet, and a month after closing when our flooring material finally arrived—in pieces—we sent it back (for a full refund) and contracted with another company, causing an additional four-week delay in possible move-in.

An interesting incident occurred when a private contractor laying floors in another unit allegedly flushed debris down the toilet, causing water damage in some 30 units in the building, including ours. Fortunately, our unit was empty, and little damage occurred. Other unit owners who had fully decorated their units were not so lucky and sustained massive damages. The developer took the position that it was not his responsibility, since the damage was caused by a private contractor working for an individual owner. It was therefore up to the association (which was already in existence) and the private owners and their insurance companies to work out the damages.

In reality, the developer did see to it that the damages to the units were repaired to the extent that water was removed from the units and drywall was replaced. However, the developer balked at paying for damages sustained to already-furnished apartments. Was the developer legally correct? Actually, he was. Recall that in a condominium, you, the purchaser, are responsible for damages to the interior of your unit. You are also responsible for damages that you or your contractors cause to others while working in your unit, unless it can be demonstrated that the proximate cause of the damages to the other units was somehow related to a construction defect in the common elements, such as faulty insulation or insufficient waterproofing. None of this was evident in this case.

Fortunately, the developer wished to avoid a scandal, and although the damages were handled as a private matter involving the unit owners, the association and their respective insurance companies, the developer made every effort to assist in minimizing the problem. However, many of the unit owners suffered as a result of this problem.

In our example, the developer still had a significant interest in the project because there were several other buildings under construction. However, it is just as likely that two years later, someone could leave the water running in a bathtub and cause the same damage, and there is no developer who will help out. In that case, it would be entirely up to the respective insurance companies to work out the damages and compensation. If you don't have homeowners insurance, then you could be personally liable, either for damages to other units or for repairs to your own unit if you are the victim of a careless unit owner.

Teaching Point: A homeowners policy should be in place certainly

.... a rather large grain of salt.

The interesting point is that all of this mayhem has not adversely affected the prices in the building, because these are not considered major problems. In other words, be prepared for the inconveniences of construction and move-in and look at the big picture. In the long run, all of this inconvenience will work itself out and you should have a beautiful home and excellent investment.

This information can be translated into other scenarios. For example:

1. *If you are going to rent your unit, be sure it is ready for the tenant's move-in date.* You don't want any delays to cause problems with your lease agreement. While you may argue that some delays are beyond your control and therefore void the contract, the idea of rental income is not to avoid damages associated with a breach of lease, but rather to actually rent the unit to a happy tenant and collect rent. Again, proper planning is the key.

2. *If you have purchased a resale unit in an already completed building, you may still encounter similar problems.* Coordination with management and knowledge of the rules are still key. If you are redecorating the unit, you will need to consider that you have neighbors who are not going to appreciate the noise and dust associated with your renovation. However, as long as you follow the rules of the building, it will be fine. Decorating and renovation are discussed in more detail later in the chapter.

Working with the Building Manager

At this point, you have probably already met with your building manager. This is a person you should get to know and appreciate. Building managers have a tough job. They are often underpaid and underappreciated. They are sometimes seen as obstacles to the free and unfettered use of your property and as always saying no to your requests. Part of the job of the building manager is to carry out and enforce the mandates of the board of directors of the association of your building. The building manager reports directly to the board, not to you.

Many condominium or co-op owners have the misguided idea that since they are owners, the manager and every member of the staff must obey their commands. This is not true. Oft times, politicians talk about the benefits of living in a free society. Obviously, neither the United States, nor any other democratic nation is truly a free society in the literal sense. Every day, we operate within rules and regulations.

Think of a condominium, cooperative, or other community association as microcosms of our democratic society. As a citizen of that society, to wit, an owner of a unit and member of the association, you have certain rights within those rules by which the association operates. As in a democratic society, you have the right to legally challenge those rules if you feel they violate statutory law—that is, the laws of the state in which the association operates, or the association documents, which are the community's constitution. However, until you successfully do so, you have no right to disobey those rules. That is the essence of community living and one that a surprising number of people do not comprehend. Understanding this fundamental concept and operating within its confines will allow you to enjoy your investment rather than have it be a source of exasperation.

DECORATING YOUR UNIT

We have already discussed the fact that you may need to get permits and permissions to do certain decorating functions in your unit. Soundproofing requirements of the association have to be followed when laying floors and plumbing electrical permits have to be obtained in certain instances. But what about colors and design? Should you paint your entire apartment orchid?

There are two schools of thought here, depending on what you are going to do with your unit. Let us assume that you are going to live in the apartment. The first school of thought is that it is your home and you should decorate to personal taste and enjoyment. The other school suggests that every property is an investment, and it should be treated as such. In the latter theory, painting your unit orchid would probably not be a wise decorating choice from an investment standpoint. Conventional decorating wisdom suggests that decorating should be done in fairly neutral tones to have maximum appeal. Of course, you could paint your unit orchid and then if you wish to sell it, redecorate.

Here's how we learned our lesson. Several years ago, a movie was being shot on location in Miami. At that time, we were of the opinion that our home is our castle and we would paint our castle any way we pleased. Our bedroom was blue, our living room was green, the bathrooms were lavender, and I can't remember what other colors we had in there. Everyone told us that they preferred more subdued tones, but we didn't listen. One day, the movie people came to our building and wanted to shoot a scene in one of the units. Ours was considered but rejected in favor of a unit that was painted—you guessed it—beige. Oh yes, the fee for using the unit for a one day shoot was $5,000. We finally got the message and painted the unit off-white. Suddenly, everyone liked the unit and we eventually sold it at a very good profit. In our opinion, neutral is better.

Local Preferences

The old adage of "when in Rome, do as the Romans do" is good advice. If you live in Florida, don't decorate the place with heavy New York style furniture, and vice versa. Keep within the style of the area where you are living. One day we were leaving the building when we noticed toilets, sinks, and bidets stacked for removal. The owner told us that she wanted an open-style apartment and she and her husband only needed one bedroom and one bathroom, as opposed to the original three-bedroom, three-bath provided for in the original unit. Two years later when she wanted to sell, she asked, "Do you think it will command less as a one-bedroom, one-bath?" Of course, the answer is yes. We don't believe that rooms should ever be removed. We believe that it does reduce the value of the unit.

Our friends' unit is unique and beautiful, but will be more difficult to sell because they have reduced the pool of prospects to a few who share their eclectic tastes. Further, it would cost a fortune to transform this unit back to original configurations. This is not to argue that if you buy a condominium-style property, you are condemned to live in a drab environment. Quite the contrary, put your decorative mark on your property—just don't go overboard to the point where if you decide to lease or sell it, it is going to appeal to a more limited market.

NOTE: If you are buying the unit to lease, your decorative touch is not an issue. Paint it white and put in a durable floor or carpet.

Hiring Contractors

While we are on the topic of decorating, let us discuss a little bit more about what you may expect to encounter in that arena. We have already discussed permitting and following the rules of the association. Unless you are a real do-it-yourselfer and you have an inordinate amount of time and limitless energy, you are going to have to hire contractors to do your work. If you are new to the area, you are going to have to find good, reliable, and cost-effective contractors to paint, lay floors, or do whatever else you may need to make the apartment livable. As we have already discussed, all contractors should be licensed and insured.

Earlier in the chapter, we relayed the story of a company that was hired to install marble in a new unit and one of the workers disposed of all the excess cement and marble chips by flushing them down the guest toilet. This caused a backup that flooded not only the owner's apartment, but also 30 units throughout the building, some of which were completely furnished. One had wood floors which had to be completely replaced.

The company was licensed and insured, and the owner did not sustain monetary damages. However, if this occurred with Uncle Fred and his drinking buddies who were "handy guys" but not licensed contractors, the owner would have been personally liable to the owners of the 30 other apartments, because the proximate cause of the damage was the negligence of the owner's agents. It is safe to assume that Uncle Fred and his buddies are not going to be able to pay to repair 30 apartments. Neither, for that matter, are those guys you met in the basement unloading a truck who do work "on the side," really cheap.

Obtaining Permits

Many local governments require that when certain types of renovations are performed, permits must be obtained. In essence, a *permit* is permission from the local government to perform the work. There are permit fees associated with this event, and sometimes, the permitting agency will require architectural plans, especially where structural changes occur.

The reason for the permitting process is to

g— -- ----— ... .u.....u.. o. nooring as well. In addition, the community association may require your contractors to submit proof that they are licensed and insured. This is to ensure that if there are any damages to the building's common elements, the contractors, or, more precisely, their insurance companies, can be held accountable.

Basically, condominiums, co-ops, and townhouses are not fertile grounds for do-it-yourself plumbers or electricians, for the reasons we just discussed. You will find that the dollars you save by using Uncle Pete, who is a car salesman by profession but "very handy around the house," or sneaking in an unlicensed person to do your electrical or plumbing work may pale in comparison to the bill you get from the association if you short out the building's electrical system or cause a flood in other people's apartments. Even if you have homeowners insurance, the insurance company may deny any claims on the basis of the fact that you used unlicensed workers. It is just not worth the risk.

Sometimes, even licensed contractors don't want to waste time going to the local government to apply for permitting, possibly having to submit architectural plans and obtaining permissions of the community association, and paying fees that they would have to pass on to you but would cause their bid on the work to go up. Some contractors will tempt you to avoid the permit process, or worse, ask you to obtain the permits in your own name. Never do this. If the permit is obtained in your name, you are solely on record as being directly liable with regard to the local government or the association should anything go wrong with the project. If your contractor obtains the permit, liability may attach to you as the owner, but the contractor as the permit holder will be directly liable as well to the local government and association. If your contractor is going to do the work, his name should go on the permit.

OBTAINING THE PROPER INSURANCE

Many clients have argued that they don't need homeowners insurance because the building has insurance and that is enough. Why spend extra money? Because you have to be fully covered. You are responsible for the interior of your unit; therefore, the building's policy generally won't cover damages that occur within the walls of your apartment.

In the example we have been discussing regarding the flooded apartments, would your homeowners insurance cover this? Maybe, but if you were using unlicensed personnel, it might give the insurance company an excuse to say you violated the law or the rules of the association and, as a result, the terms of your insurance policy. Insurance companies are not charitable organizations, either. In reality, the burden of proof is often on the insured to prove that he should be paid, and the insurance company often takes the initial position that it does not have to pay. The friendly insurance agent portrayed on television who comes running with a check and chocolate chip cookies at the first sign of trouble is somewhat of an exaggeration. Although some insurance companies are very good, there are certain formalities that must be followed. Insurance companies have to investigate, and adjusters have to verify the damages and amounts to be paid. We've had some very good experiences with insurance companies, but in no case did my agent come racing to my condominium at breakneck speeds, waving cash and cookies.

READ AND HEED: Even if the proximate cause of the damage to the interior of your unit results from a common element problem, the buildings insurance may still not cover the damages.

Florida has specific statutory insurance regulations that dictate what a condominium policy may or may not pay for damages caused by a common-element problem, such as a leak in a water pipe within the common elements of the building. For example, if a common-element water pipe bursts, causing damage to your unit, Florida condominium insurance law indicates that the building's policy may pay for damages to your kitchen cabinets, but only if they were the original kitchen cabinets installed by the developer prior to a certain date. In addition, in areas with severe weather problems, such as hurricanes or extreme winters, damage to individual units will not be covered by the building's insurance policies.

Insurance for Acts of Nature

There are some types of insurance you may not need. For example, if you live on the twenty-fifth floor of a condominium complex, you probably

you it may wise to purchase windstorm insurance. This is essentially hurricane insurance. Remember, the building's policies probably will not cover damages to the interior of your unit, so if you live in an area that is prone to severe weather such as hurricanes, you may wish to make such a purchase. The problem with windstorm insurance is that it is expensive and, especially in Florida, few if any companies will write such a policy. The federal government will underwrite these types of policies, but they require the entire premium be paid up front. This could easily run about $2,000. However, considering the devastating effects of hurricanes, it is well worth it, and you should be prepared to budget for it.

Appliance Insurance

What other types of insurance are available? We would recommend appliance insurance. Minimally, you are going to have a variety of kitchen appliances in your unit, including a refrigerator, an oven, a dishwasher, perhaps a washer and dryer, maybe a microwave. If you bought the apartment directly from the developer, these appliances may be covered for up to a year and individual policies offered by the appliance company may be available. However, these can be expensive and may not cover other items, such as air conditioning.

There are many reputable companies that offer comprehensive appliance repair contracts at very affordable rates. Usually, the company will send an inspector to check your appliances and air conditioning unit and will issue a policy. They can run anywhere from about $150 and up per year, depending on coverage required. Most of these policies state that if they can't repair an appliance, they will replace it with a similar one. This can prove to be very valuable.

One summer, our building experienced a power outage, which damaged some of the air conditioning units in the apartments. This, of course, occurred on a weekend. Our neighbor did not have any type of insurance and complained to the building manager. The manager patiently and correctly explained that there was no responsibility on the part of the management to repair private air conditioning units within the owner's units. Our neighbor was advised to call the air conditioning repair service number found on the air conditioning unit. Unfortunately, that company did not work on weekends and offered no emergency service. Our neighbor located a company that did emergency services on weekends and the air conditioner was repaired, but at monumental cost.

We called our appliance company, and for a small extra charge a technician came on the weekend and replaced the damaged parts. The moral of the story is that it cost our neighbor more money for the one emergency visit than we paid for the appliance contract for the year. Sooner or later, you are going to encounter problems with appliances, and when that happens, you are going to be glad you carried some sort of repair policy.

If you are leasing your unit, unless you have a degree in mechanical engineering and love to visit your tenants, you will definitely want an appliance policy.

PAYING SPECIAL ASSESSMENTS

You have moved into your apartment and are enjoying your new investment. You attend your monthly board meetings and all appears to be good. One day you check your mail and you receive a notice that there is going to be a special meeting of the board of directors to discuss and vote on a special assessment. Although you are not sure exactly what a special assessment is, it sounds like it is going to cost you money. You are absolutely right.

A *special assessment* is a charge to the unit owners for some special project which the building requires that was not accounted for in the annual budget. It is usually some one-time repair or maintenance of the property such as painting the building or repairing some construction defect. It might also be for a *capital improvement* such as the addition of a tennis court or new gym equipment.

The condominium documents indicate what authority the board of directors has with regard to passing special assessments, but in most cases, it is up to the board of directors to maintain the building, and if there is not enough money allocated in the budget, then they have the authority to pass a special assessment. (See Chapter 6 for more on the board of directors.)

Generally speaking, a board of directors, who are almost always residents of the building and, thus, also have to pay these monies, will make

decision is made to make the purchase, the board will pass the special assessment.

The condominium documents dictate what percentage each unit owner will have to pay. Most condominiums are based on a percentage of the square footage of the unit. However, other condominiums pay based on the number of bedrooms or the floor they are on, or a combination of both. As a rule of thumb, the larger your unit, the more you are going to have to pay.

The problem with special assessments is that, although necessary for the maintenance of the building and the preservation of the value of the building, they can have short-term negative effects. Prospective buyers must be informed that a special assessment has been passed by the board of directors or is in progress. A building undergoing a special assessment could have a chilling effect on potential buyers who do not wish to incur additional expense. If the seller knows or even suspects that a special assessment is forthcoming, but it has not yet been scheduled as an agenda item at a board of directors meeting, there is generally no legal obligation to disclose this to a buyer. It is not certain that the board will actually place the special assessment on the agenda. Once it is an agenda item, however, there is a duty to disclose it. We will discuss this aspect in greater detail in Chapter 10, Selling the Property.

For now, understand that it may be necessary from time to time to pay special assessments in order to perform either upkeep or capital improvements on the property. As suggested earlier, there is a difference between a capital improvement and a repair or maintenance project. A capital improvement creates something that was not there before. For example, if the building had no swimming pool and one is built, that is a capital improvement. If the building has a swimming pool but the automatic chlorinator must be repaired or replaced, that is a repair or maintenance project.

Depending on the board of director's authority granted in the condominium documents, there may be a difference in what the board may approve without a vote of the members. Generally, boards will have up to a certain amount of money per year to approve capital improvements and unlimited authority to approve repair and maintenance projects. The percentage of votes necessary to approve a capital improvement project depends on the authority granted in the condominium documents.

Figuring out the Rules

Association rules and regulations may restrict what you can do within the common elements of the building as well as within your own interior unit. Although we have already discussed issues such as pets and use of the amenities, there are other matters you need to be concerned with. Issues such as placement of satellite dishes, loud music and television, and children and pets will be issues that will confront you from time to time in a community association atmosphere.

Satellite Dishes

One of the more controversial rules is the use and placement of satellite dishes. Satellite dishes are battling cable companies for control of the airwaves. The satellite companies contend that they deliver more channels worldwide, with greater GEEWHIZ technology, while the cable companies counter that a good rainstorm will cause interference of service and cable reception is the best, cheapest, and most reliable. I don't know who is right, but for this discussion, we will focus on the problems that satellite dishes have created.

One problem is that they are often bulky and unsightly. Also, they must be placed in certain positions to reach their signals. If they have to be placed facing east and your apartment faces west, you may have a problem. What satellite companies have done was simply screw the dish onto the side of the building and run wires to the client's apartment. Some buildings began to resemble the Pentagon. Since most condominium documents did not contemplate this problem, it was not addressed in the rules.

When associations attempted to have the dishes removed, they argued that the owners placed the dishes on the common elements of the building without consent of the board and had no right to do so. That was essentially correct, but the satellite companies did not give in so easily. They argued that the associations, whose rights were at best granted by state laws, had no authority to restrict satellite signals, which are governed by federal law. While basically a technical argument, it was a very good technical argu-

the terrace on the floor and it can't overhang the railing. There has been some delegated authority to the local governments to further regulate the placement of satellite dishes on buildings. Those rules usually mimic the common-element rules of basic condominium law.

The Noise Issue

Another problem you may encounter in community association life is noise. We have already addressed this earlier, but as it is a very common issue, it deserves a bit more analysis. The ancient, albeit politically incorrect rule of home ownership is, "A man's home is his castle." Substitute "person" for "man" and "condominium apartment" for castle, and you have the same basic rule of law, but with many more complications. Essentially, and very obviously, a twenty-first-century apartment is not a castle. So if you have a party, or you play your music too loud, you are going to disturb your neighbor, whose only noise protection is whatever the local building code says is the minimum required sound insulation. Usually, the local zoning ordinances state when undue or unreasonable noise must cease; prior to that time, the police are reluctant to get involved in noise disputes.

Personally, we disagree. The key is what constitutes *unreasonable noise,* and this is very subjective. What if your neighbor likes to play his or her television at top volume all day long? This sounds unreasonable. What about if your next-door neighbor has a hearing problem and must play the television very loud in order to hear it? Is it still unreasonable? What about if you have unusually acute hearing?

The legal answer is based on what is generally considered the "reasonable person" standard. Would a reasonable person consider the noise to be disturbing or offensive? If we apply it to the example concerning the playing of the television, the answer should be that playing the television at full blast all day long is *not* reasonable. Although it may sound a bit unfeeling, the fact is that the reasonable person test applies based on a person with normal hearing, not a reasonable deaf person or a reasonable person with acute hearing sensitivity. A person with reasonable hearing should play the television at a reasonable volume.

Thus, if your upstairs neighbor throws a party for 50 people with a rock band, that is probably not reasonable, no matter what time the party takes place. However, the result may be different if that same neighbor has a party in the afternoon and you can hear people laughing. The fact is, new construction is no match for new music technology. Super bass systems will cause reverberations throughout a building, and there isn't much that can be done about it. For me, there is nothing worse than a vibrating bass from some neighbor's stereo.

Children and Pets

Children and pets are the other perennial problem that merits some discussion. Mark Twain said that there is no such thing as a bad child, only bad parents. I don't know if Twain was right or wrong, but I tend to think he was certainly headed in the right direction.

Parents and pet owners have rights, but so do non-parents and non–pet owners. If there is a rule prohibiting children under a certain age from using an amenity, that rule should be either respected or the parent should try to get it changed. The same goes for pets. If there is a rule that indicates that pets must be handled in a certain manner, follow the rules.

You may think your screaming child is the cutest thing, but someone else may not. I recall an incident in a building I lived in with a rule that children without waterproof diapers are not permitted in the swimming pool. Obviously, the parent of this particular infant felt that this rule pertained to children other than her own, and she placed her child in the pool, where he promptly did his business out of both ends. The pool had to be closed while regulations concerning the treating of the water under those conditions were met. I can tell you that parent felt no remorse at all and couldn't understand what all the fuss was about, even though it necessitated the closing of the pool in middle of the summer in south Florida. After all, it was just a little baby poo. I've changed babies, and baby poo isn't cute and it isn't pleasant. I don't want to swim in it, thank you very much.

People love their children and their pets. I've known people who treat their pets as a family equal. They can't understand how rules can be placed on their pets. They're okay for other people's mongrels, but not their Lassie.

Dealing with Your Neighbors

exposing yourself to abuse from the neighbor. In many cases, the manager will be able to resolve the issue, and you will have gone through the proper channels to voice your complaint.

Be prepared to get this argument from the offending party: "Why didn't you just come to me and say something? You didn't have to go to the manager." This argument is designed to put you on the defensive, to imply that you, not they, are the rude and offending party, and to transfer some aspect of guilt to you. Forget it! Simply reply that you don't know him or her well, and that you don't like to be confrontational with strangers. Also, you wanted to get a reading on the rule to make sure that you were in the right. Once the manager agreed, he or she indicated the intention to take care of the problem, which is the manager's job. Then simply walk away. Sometimes, after the dispute is settled, you may even become friends with this person—but don't count on it.

The Condo Commando

We should not leave our discussion of living in a condominium without an honorable mention of that ubiquitous person who, in one guise or another, is always found in a condominium (or any other community living situation), the condo commando—self-proclaimed superhero of condominium dwellers.

The condo commando is usually a person who always seems to be where you don't need him or her. The person knows every rule by heart and always seems to be around when you are breaking one, no matter how small and seemingly insignificant. Your first thought when encountering such a person is, "Get a life." But if you think about it, the condominium *is* his or her life. So if a condo commando catches you breaking some rule, smile, be apologetic (it won't help), take the inevitable tongue-lashing lecture, and move on. Don't even bother arguing.

Sooner or later, the condo commando will be on your side in some other dispute. Enjoy that person and don't get aggravated. There's at least one in every building.

Community Living Is About Courtesy

At the end of the day, community living is not based on interpretations of legal tests, but on the courtesy of neighbors living in a community. Technology is not going away. Stereos are getting smaller and louder. People have families with small children who make noise. Dogs bark. Years ago, I recall living underneath a couple who were getting a divorce. They fought loudly and endlessly each and every night, and I felt like I was going through the divorce with them. Finally, the husband moved out and I could get a good night's sleep.

TEACHING POINT: The essence of community living is courtesy. There is an old expression stating that you should be nice to people on the way up, because you will see them again on the way down. This is good advice for everyone, but especially people living together in a common community.

The fact is, if you demand freedom to act as you please, condominium living may not be for you. A private home may be the way to go.

However, while you will certainly encounter these types of problems with residential community living, for the most part they should be isolated incidents. A bad neighbor is a problem no matter what type of living accommodation you choose. But, if handled properly, most problems you will encounter in a condominium or other community association will be of a temporary nature and condominium or community association living will be a pleasurable and profitable experience.

In Chapter 10, we are going to address the selling of condominium property. This is where the real profit comes into play. For now, you should know basically what it is to live in a condominium atmosphere. If you know what to expect, you will be better prepared to move within the societal norms of the building. My wife and I enjoy condominium living. It affords us a lifestyle that we couldn't aspire to if we had a private home, plus our investments appreciate in value.

CHAPTER 10

This is it, the moment of truth. If, indeed, all property is an investment, as we have argued thus far, then selling the property is when the investment pays off, and it should. In this chapter, we will look at the decision to sell, preparations for the sale, marketing the property, and closing the sale.

DECIDING TO SELL

You have come full circle with your investment, and now you want to sell it. What factors should you consider in making the decision to sell? If you can't carry the property or you need the money (i.e., you need to free up capital) for whatever reason, the decision is already made, you have to sell. But let us suppose that the scenario is different. Let us suppose that you can either hold the property or sell it as you wish, but you need to consider if this is the right time. There are a number of factors you should be considering.

The main issue is the real estate market in your area. In plain, everyday language, the market is either hot, flat, or bad. A hot real estate market, which is a seller's market, means the property is rising in value. Demand is high and the supply is low, or at least lower than the demand. As this book is being written, some of the hot real estate markets in the country for condominiums are Manhattan, Las Vegas, and almost anywhere in Florida.

The trick in a hot real estate market, as in any other investment, is to know when to hold and know when to fold.

The popular phrase being bantered about today is "the imminent bursting real estate bubble." So, employing the current vernacular, how do you know when the bubble is going to burst?

Unfortunately, you don't. Nobody does. You do the best you can with the information you have. That is why investing is an art as well as a science. All you can do is watch for indications.

What Makes a Market Hot?

The first question you have to ask is, what makes the particular market "hot"? What is the driving force or forces behind the surge in real estate prices? Florida, for example, has the weather, and the fact that it is regarded as a vacation paradise. The cost of living is regarded as being cheaper. It is also very popular among foreign investors, which means it attracts new capital, especially from the former Russian republic, Europe, and from Central and South America.

Hot markets also help to sustain themselves. If there is a demand for condominiums, builders will build them. This translates into jobs. Jobs for architects, construction workers, real estate brokers, mortgage brokers, decorators, retail sales for food, clothing, supplies, insurance, automotive (car sales)—the list goes on and on. As more people arrive seeking work, there is additional need for housing at all levels, which helps propagate the overall economy as well. This is exactly what is happening in Florida.

In New York City, the real estate market has been traditionally strong. Even in the wake of 9/11, the market recovered quickly and is back on track. There have been very few periods in New York City's history when the market was flat, or bad. What has New York City to offer? It is a world center for commerce and culture. Simply put, it has everything for everyone. If you want to live in Manhattan, you have to pay the price.

What about Las Vegas? Once regarded as a center for gambling and sex, it reinvented itself as a family resort town with nongambling hotels and family-style entertainment such as theme parks and circus-type shows. People began to rediscover Las Vegas for all manner of entertainment, not just adult activities, and developers began to look at it for condominiums and hotel-condominiums. It is now enjoying a rebirth, with thousands of people coming to find jobs to support all facets of the city's economic life.

Supply and Demand

We know that an active real estate market is a good thing. But we still don't know what predictors can cause it to turn flat or bad. Let's begin

have no desire to ever occupy the property they buy, eventually, supply will outweigh demand. This may first be reflected in the real estate rental market. If there are an abundance of rental properties on the market, this may be an indication that there are too many investor-type units on the market and they are not being absorbed.

Investors who can't rent their units and either can't or don't wish to carry them empty until they appreciate sufficiently place them on the market for resale. If too many of these properties hit the marketplace for resale, there will be too much supply for the demand and housing prices will decline.

Reaching a Price Ceiling

There is a secondary issue associated with the problem of selling condominiums. In a hot real estate market, investors can make upwards of 100 percent profit, depending on the price they originally paid for their property. However, sellers tend not to be objective about their investments and often demand that profit too quickly. What happens in these cases is that an investor will purchase a unit and close, hoping to lease the apartment for income while it is appreciating. Short of living in the unit, that is the highest and best possible use of the property. However, to get upwards of 100 percent profit on an investment in a condominium, you must wait.

Real estate is not a liquid asset. It takes time to appreciate, even in a hot real estate market. An anxious seller who can't rent his or her property will often list it for sale, but with the expectation of garnering 100 percent profit immediately. So the seller lists too high and the property doesn't sell. This sends out a message that the real estate market is cooling off. It is not necessarily cooling off, but rather, it has reached its ceiling in terms of price range on the high end.

That same person, if he or she truly wishes to grab a quick profit, say 15 percent on average, and move on, will probably be able to sell the unit in short order. This brings us to the hot real estate market phenomena known as *flipping*.

Flipping Your Property

Flipping units, or more precisely, flipping contracts, simply means that you purchase a condominium from a developer and sell your rights to close on the unit to another party for a profit prior to actually closing on the unit. The profits range, on average, from 10 to 30 percent of the purchase price, depending on how well the property you invest in is doing, or how strong the demand is for that property. There are really only two important points you must remember in purchasing a property for flipping:

1. Does the developer allow it?

2. If for any reason you cannot flip the property, can you close and carry the unit for six months to a year to give you time to sell the property?

From an investment standpoint, flipping presents itself as a wonderful opportunity to purchase high-priced properties with a small down payment and sell them at an excellent short-term profit. For example on a $400,000 property, an investor would put down $80,000 (20% deposit) and, in a hot market, within a year could flip the contract for a 30 percent profit of the purchase price. That is, $80,000 invested would provide a $120,000 profit—i.e., a 150 percent return on the investment!

READ AND HEED: This is highly risky because if for any reason you can't flip the property and you can't close on it and carry it, you will lose your investment capital.

Easy Financing

The availability of credit is another factor that contributes to a hot real estate market. We have seen in Chapter 8 the importance of financing. As this book is being written, interest rates are rising slowly—in fact, we count 14 times over the last four years. However, they are still in the lowest range they have been for the last four decades. Also, the Fed seems inclined to slowly move these rates to a reasonable level to neither chill the market and thereby damage consumer confidence with double-digit rates, nor hurt the economy by encouraging ~~overheating~~ ~~~~ ~~~~

~~~~ ~~~~ ~~~~ ~~~~ ~~~~ a ~~hot~~ real estate market is coming to an end—or, as the popular term is now being used, that the bubble will burst?

We have already discussed the laws of supply and demand. Once supply exceeds demand, the market softens, or, in money terms, the prices of units are forced down. This does not happen immediately. Sellers are often slow to recognize, or refuse to accept, that the market has softened and refuse to lower their prices to more realistic levels. This causes property prices to remain high, with sellers refusing to lower prices and buyers refusing to pay the prices. If such a stalemate occurs, the hot market begins to cool.

In addition, real estate markets, like the stock market, are susceptible to outside factors. For example, if the interest rates begin to rise, people may react by buying sooner before rates go any higher, in which case there will be a flurry of activity, but then as the rates begin to rise in earnest, investors will wait until rates stabilize before making further purchases. This often has the effect of cooling the real estate market.

Other factors that can contribute to a real estate downturn include political or economic changes in foreign countries whose citizens are investing in United States real estate. Changes in the exchange rates could affect the ability or desire of foreigners to invest in United States real property. Right now, a weak U.S. dollar makes investments in U.S. real estate very attractive to citizens of countries with stronger currencies. But what if that changes?

A very strong U.S. dollar could discourage investors from further investment. It may also make carrying those properties including payment of mortgages, assessments, and taxes too great a burden. In that case, foreign investors may decide to sell their apartments, thereby placing more product on the market to weigh in on the supply side, where the demand for such property by their countrymen is now reduced or eliminated. Sometimes, a foreign country may have a change in government, and the new administration decides to restrict the amount of money that can be invested abroad. This would also hinder investment in United States real estate.

Other factors that can adversely affect a real estate market involve the local economy. If an area is dependent on a local industry and that industry disappears, the economy of the area can be shattered. For example, large factories or military bases often sustain communities, including their real estate market, and the effect can be devastating on an area if they close. It can take years before a real estate market recovers. Does this mean that one should not invest in real estate? Of course not.

The Long-Term Benefits of Real Estate

The real estate market has proven itself over time to be remarkably resilient and is far less volatile than the stock market. Almost any type of news, positive or negative, can affect the stock market on a daily basis. Real estate reacts far more slowly. Military base and factory closures aside, a rise in the interest rates will not send the real estate market into a slump. Record high prices of gasoline have not destroyed consumer confidence. The terrorist attacks of 9/11 did not destroy the real estate market in New York, and people continue to invest in real estate throughout the United States at tremendous profits. In addition, severe hurricanes in Florida have not destroyed their real estate market.

Recall that at the onset of this book, when we dealt with the purchase of condominiums, cooperatives, and townhouses, we recommended that you do research in accordance with what we described as A.P.E.—area, perception, and economics. Thus, when making your purchase, you would have considered what factors sustain the area, as well as many other factors that we have already described.

TEACHING POINT: The primary rule in real estate is that over time, real estate appreciates rather than depreciates. The other rule involved in real estate investing is that, generally speaking, real estate tends not to be a liquid asset.

Recently, we sold a condominium for a client in six days. However, the transaction took about 40 days in total to complete and the investor held the property for about a year and a half from the time she purchased it from the developer to the time of sale. She closed on the property, improved it, and then listed it for sale with our firm. The process went very quickly and on schedule, but you can see that it was not a phone call to a stockbroker, with a check in the mail or wire transfer to your account the following day. Not being liquid has its advantages, however. In the same token as you cannot cash in your chips immediately ~~~~ ~

~~~ ~~~~ ~~~~ ~~~~ ~~~~ ~~~~ current real estate boom in the United States. One magazine featured side-by-side "expert" opinions. On the left column was a doom and gloom article predicting an imminent real estate bursting bubble. On the right-hand column, the other expert was writing how he was investing every asset he had in real estate, and that there were absolutely no signs of the good times rolling to an end. Who's right? Who knows? That is why it is an investment. The greater the risk, the greater the revenue but the greater the possibility of equally greater losses. There is some advice that we can offer to help you read the market trends:

1. *Be careful not to overgeneralize.* There are general trends and site-specific trends in real estate. For example, as we write this book, overall, the United States is enjoying a real estate "boom" market. There are certain factors that contribute to this, such as low interest rates, and the fact that the stock market is sluggish and banks are giving very low interest rates on savings and certificates of deposits. There is very little in the investment community that can compare with the high real estate yields and generally low risks, as opposed to investing in the stock market.

These indicators hold true in Bismarck, North Dakota, Miami Beach, Florida, and Los Angeles, California. Conversely, the residential housing market in Bismarck, North Dakota, has little to do with the condominium market in south Florida, or Vale, Colorado. So each area must be analyzed as well (remember our A.P.E. formula).

On one hand, if you are the owner of a home next to an Air Force base that just closed, or an automobile factory that just relocated, your housing bubble may have indeed burst, at least for the near future. On the other hand, if you are the owner of a condominium in south Florida, you may be happily decorating your unit in hopes of a nice rental income or a nice double- or triple-digit profit. Your real estate bubble is floating away and all is right with the world. The teaching point is to watch both nationwide and local trends to help you attempt to predict the market.

2. *Be flexible.* Don't fall in love with your investment. We repeat again and again, real estate is an investment and should be treated as such. You have to look at the entire picture objectively. Sometimes, the signs are so clear that they hit you in the face and you refuse to believe it.

We were watching a condominium investment in London for a client of ours. We advised him to sell before the market took a downturn. He told us that we "colonials" don't understand the British property market and should stick to our own shores. The problem was that the British government decided that the real estate market in Great Britain was so "hot" that young people (who are beginning to represent a large voting block) couldn't afford to buy new homes. Rather than put programs in place to provide affordable housing, they mounted a campaign to lower the price of property across the board.

Each day, the chairman of the Bank of England, or some other top executive, would make some "doom and gloom" pronouncement about the risks of property speculation. We read these articles and watched as the Bank of England began to raise the interest rates. The British government succeeded in scaring investors and finally caused the market to pretty much collapse. This not only affected housing prices, but retail sales and the British economy in general, as it affected consumer confidence and retail spending, as well as jobs related to the housing market.

Our client in London? He leased his condominium and is collecting nice rental income, but has elected to wait until the market recuperates before selling. The teaching point is simply that sometimes, the signs are so obvious that they hit you in the face and you don't see them because you can't imagine that your property will be affected. We saw it coming. It was obvious to us as outsiders but not to the client, who couldn't come to grips with the fact that anything could affect such a strong property market.

Just to confuse you a bit more, we recently read a newspaper article about a couple living in New York City. They owned a luxury condominium in Manhattan and were enjoying watching the value of their investment go up. They apparently read a number of imminent doom and gloom articles about the real estate bubble bursting and decided to take action, sell, rent for a while, and wait for the bubble to burst, and then make a purchase of a larger apartment at a depressed price. It seemed a good plan. They quickly sold their condominium for a handsome profit and leased an apartment while they waited for the market to drop. Unfortunately, the market hasn't dropped, but instead has continued to rise dram...

...g. Are there exceptions? Of course, but if you don't take any risks you don't make any money. "No guts, no glory" is as true in the real estate market as it is on the battlefield. A solid investment will yield the greatest return and will better weather the downturns as well.

One of my favorite stories involves a repairman who came to service our air conditioner. We began to talk and he told us how much he loved real estate. "You know," he said, "My wife and I bought our house 25 years ago. We raised two children and refinanced it a dozen times as it continued to appreciate. We put our kids through college, bought them cars, and generally got them started in life. Now that they are moving out, we are selling the place and are going to buy a condominium with the equity." That is truly the highest and best use of real estate.

A Personal Story on Real Estate Trends

Before moving on to the preparation for the sale of a condominium, we'll end the discussion of real estate trends and the decision to sell property with this story. Twenty-five years ago, my wife and I were starting out in real estate. We bought three properties in the northern Florida panhandle. Two were close to the ocean in a golfing community and the third was in the middle of nowhere, but with beautiful trees and wildlife. All three were extremely cheap with negligible taxes, as they were undeveloped land.

The beautiful tree community did nothing for 25 years, while the golf community was a tremendous success. We sold the golf property years ago at a small profit. My wife chided me for years about holding our beautiful but apparently worthless property and pushing to sell the golf property, for which we could have made far more money had we held it longer. However, lately the beautiful property has dramatically risen threefold in value and continues to go up. So now I have foresight and vision because I believed in the wooded property.

Was it vision and foresight? Hardly—the property came into its own, as real estate tends to do, eventually. These trends apply to condominiums, co-ops, and townhouses as well.

PREPARING TO SELL

If your time has come to sell your condominium, how do you prepare for the sale? How do you know what the price should be? Do you need a real estate broker or an attorney? What preparations should you make with regard to repairing or upgrading your property? What is the best way to advertise it?

What's the Property Worth?

You have made the decision to sell your condominium. What is the first thing you should do? The obvious answer is to find out what you think the property is worth. This is not as simple as you may think.

The generally accepted method of pricing a condominium, cooperative, or townhouse is for the owner to go to the swimming pool, lobby, or other social area and discuss the matter with his or her neighbors. This is the worst possible way to conduct research and will almost guarantee failure in your sales endeavor. For one thing, people tend to have an overinflated estimate of the value of their property. "Don't worry; list it for a zillion dollars, I know one guy who sold it in a week at that price. He cleaned up," your neighbor will tell you.

What your neighbor doesn't factor is that the "guy" who got a zillion dollars actually didn't get anywhere near that much, and owned the best and largest apartment in another, more expensive condominium, had it highly upgraded, and his sale was in no way comparable to your one-bedroom, one-and-one-half-bath on the fifth floor that hasn't been improved since you made the purchase ten years ago. Rumors are not what you need—you need facts.

There are many ways to acquire facts when it comes to selling a condominium, or any property for that matter. Getting the right facts is equally important. So where do you start?

Listing Price and Closed Sales

Listing prices are the price a property is advertised at, and closed prices—the prices that a property actually sold for—are public knowledge. There are numerous real estate web sites that provide information on listed property and closed sales. Also, if you are not such a techie, a trip to a local real estate broker will provide you with all the information you will require. Brokers generally give out this information for a few a

beachfront community. Your building is located across the street from the beach on the fifteenth floor. Although your unit faces the ocean, the only reason you can see the ocean is because the lot across the street is empty. The lot is owned by the city, and it was supposed to build a park on the property but the project never materialized. There is a rumor that the city is going to sell the lot to a developer to build a high-rise condominium, which will entirely block your ocean view. However, the city has not consummated any deals, and no immediate plans or permits have been filed with the city for any construction permits.

In addition, you have owned your unit for ten years. When you purchased it, you hired a decorator and you spent $20,000 to furnish and paint it. You also placed Italian marble (12-by-12-inch squares) in the living room and white shag carpets in the bedrooms. Although you used the apartment as a second home and a seasonal rental, it has held up well. The original appliances still work. Even the wallpaper in the bathrooms is fairly clean.

You purchased the condominium for $250,000 with 30 percent down, but over the years you used the rental income to pay off chunks of the mortgage, so that there is very little remaining to pay off. The building is well maintained, but the maintenance is somewhat high for the area, due to the fact that the board has elected to pay off a recreation lease and spend on replacing the old-style elevators with new and larger high-speed computerized models. There is a special assessment of $300 per month for your unit, which will last another year.

Property values in the area have soared over the past few years. Your condominium has 200 units, of which 15 are listed for sale. There are also three other buildings on your street and six condominiums across the street, directly on the ocean, which are extremely high-end luxury units. All have apartments for sale. There is a public beach access about one block away.

Your building has a gym, swimming pool, sauna, and tennis court as its amenities. The gymnasium has the original equipment the developer placed 15 years ago, but the pool is sufficiently large to allow for swimming laps. It is clean and well maintained, but the sauna has not been well maintained.

There is a major shopping mall about five minutes from your complex by car. It has a multiplex cinema and several up-scale restaurants and a number of fast-food chains. Your property is within walking distance to two large supermarkets, a pharmacy, several banks, and a number of houses of worship for the major religions. In fact, the area is considered one of the most appealing in the city.

You discussed your decision with your neighbor, who advised you that these units are moving faster than the speed of light and if you accept anything less than $900,000 for your apartment, you are literally giving it away. Delighted with this information, you decide that you are going to employ a local broker because you can't spend the time to do it yourself. In fact, you have only a few days of vacation to set things up. Fortunately, the tenant who occupied the unit only has two more months on her lease before she goes home to Canada for the summer. You go see a local broker. You tell him that you want to list your apartment for $950,000 and you expect that in this "hot real estate market" it shouldn't take him more than a month to sell your professionally decorated unit, so you'll give only a one-month listing.

That's the scenario. What do you think? Crazy, right? Who would do such thing? The answer is, more people than you think, which is why sellers often feel frustrated and disappointed with their sales, even if they make profits in excess of 100 percent. Sellers' expectations are usually too high, and that is due to a lack of objectivity. Remember that we discussed the need to be objective about your property? Here is where it is put to the test. Let's go back and analyze the scenario in greater detail.

Getting the Right Information

Your first mistake was to discuss your sale with the neighbor. This neighbor has created, without any real facts to back it up, an unreasonable expectation in your mind. The first thing you need to do is find out what is on the market. Let's say you make a trip to the local real estate broker. What information do you initially need?

Comparable Properties. You need to look at comparable properties, or *comps*. But comps are not just a list of everything available in the area. Comps need to reflect what is available in units as closely similar to the subject unit as can be found. Suppose the~~~~~~~~~~

~~~~~,~~~ ~~~ two-bedroom, two-bath units, but they were direct oceanfront apartments across the street in new high-end ultra-luxurious properties. The seven comparable units that remained were listed between $700,000 and $850,000.

What does this scenario tell us? What price would you list the unit for? We know that no units listed over $700,000 have sold, while those in the $500,000s were sold. It is therefore a safe bet that your neighbor's appraisal of $900,000 was a bit of wishful thinking and no more. But do you have enough information to make the decision? The answer is still no. This is where objectivity comes in once again. What factors contributed to the sale of the units at the $580,000 range, as opposed to the $430,000 range?

Factors That Affect Price. There are several factors you need to consider in analyzing the sales data. One factor is view and floor level. Do the majority of the apartments face a parking lot or a beautiful mountain? Does your apartment have a panoramic view of the city with a vista of city lights at night, or does it face an alley? Are you on the third floor or the twenty-third floor?

It is important to note that of these factors and others we are going to discuss, each contributes to price but none are solely determinative in and of themselves. For example, a rule of thumb is that a developer will raise the price of a unit by $5,000 per floor, based on the presumption that the higher the floor, the better the view and, consequently, the more desirable the property is. But what if you have acrophobia? What if your religion prevents you from riding the elevator on your religious holidays? Is a twenty-third-floor apartment valuable to you? If you like city views, is a pure oceanfront apartment more valuable to you? The answer is no, but when you are selling real estate, you have to deal with the general percep-tions of the marketplace. Generally speaking, a higher floor is worth more than a lower floor and the optimum view is worth more than one facing an alleyway or another building. When selling, you have the option to wait for the person who wants a low floor and demand your price, but that may take more time than you wish. At the right price, everything sells. The question is, can you accept the right price?

What else do we know about the properties that were sold? Were they furnished or unfurnished? Furnished apartments sometimes command a higher price than unfurnished apartments but many prospects have their own furniture and are not interested in purchasing yours.

So in analyzing the prices commanded for similar units, you should be looking at floor level, views, and furnishings. Furnishings not only include furniture but types of flooring and window treatment. Obviously, you would want to know about the highest sold comparable, which was $580,000. As mentioned before, all of this information is public record and any local real estate broker will be able to supply you with this information. You may also be able to find it on the Internet if you are willing to invest the time and have the skill.

For our purposes, let's say that the unit that sold for $580,000 was a penthouse unit. Although not furnished, the owner upgraded and modernized the kitchen and bathrooms. He also recently replaced the carpets with 24-by-24-inch marble and put a fresh coat of white paint on the walls. His furniture was new and modern, and the unit was shown furnished, as opposed to empty. The view of the unit was toward the beach and directly in front of the park, so there were no obstructed views of the ocean. The unit was originally listed for $620,000 but was reduced after three months to $600,000.

Now take a look at the unit that sold at the low end for $430,000. This unit was sold in "as-is" condition. There were no improvements done by the owner, who was the original purchaser. The unit was located on the third floor of the building and faced the top level of the garage. The floors were covered in the original carpets. However, the records show the owner paid $185,000 cash for the unit. So without any improvements, he still made a very handsome profit, plus he had the unit rented to the same tenant since the day he made the purchase. In fact, one of the reasons he sold was because the tenant, who was getting on in years, elected to move in with his daughter and her family and so did not renew the lease. This information you get through the grapevine; it is not in any official records. Most brokers will know the back story involved with the sale of a property.

The units that sold in between those two extremes will generally reflect differences in floor levels, views, furnishings, and upgrades.

Determining the Price Range

ιυuι unit nas one bedroom, one full bath, and a half bath with sink and toilet but no shower. However, there is another line of units that have four apartments available with one bedroom and one bath and with less square footage but similar views. These list for about $50,000 less and people don't seem to mind that they are slightly smaller. Buyers are tempted to purchase these units to save money. The remaining units are two full bedrooms two full baths, and one half bath. They list for about $100,000 more and are not competing with your unit. The real estate market is brisk, and there is demand for units in your building.

As the seller, you have two problems. The first is determining a price and the second is how much money to invest in the unit to make it competitive with the other available units. Let us further suppose that of the other six units that directly compete with you, and the other four units that indirectly compete, five are highly upgraded with new floors and baths. Of the remaining five, three are being offered "as is" but are on higher floors. The other two are on lower floors and are not upgraded. Prices of the six directly competing units average $600,000 with a high end of $900,000 and a low end of $475,000. The unit being offered at $475,000 is on a low floor and unimproved. Of the improved units, the listed prices range in the mid-$500,000s.

A Word About Upgrades

Many of our clients tell us they don't want to invest in refurbishing their property because it may not be the taste of the prospective purchasers. An extension of that argument is that the seller does not want to upgrade because the new buyer will probably change things anyway, so it is a waste of money. Another variation of that argument is, "If the buyer wants to make an offer, he can offer with what he wants done in the apartment and I'll consider it then."

All of these arguments are wrong. The reason for upgrading an apartment is to make it competitive with other units that are also for sale. Remember, why do most developers have a model apartment for viewing? It is not because they want to spend extra money. It is because people have difficulty imagining an apartment without furniture and fixtures. Empty units, especially those with wear and tear such as carpet stains and imprints from furniture that has been placed in the same location for years, present a poor image to the prospect, as opposed to a clean and nicely furnished unit.

We owned a unit we wanted to sell. We moved our furniture out and showed the apartment empty. There was virtually no interest in it, except for really low offers. Then we decided to furnish it. We bought some nice but inexpensive furniture and gave the place a fresh coat of paint, and interest in the unit rose remarkably. We were able to sell the unit within the next two months at the fair market value.

Also, with regard to the third variation discussed, that the seller will fix the unit in accordance with the demands of the buyer, you don't want to do this even if you get an offer. For one thing, it is very hard to please buyers. They may think they are getting one grade of paint and you may wish to give another (usually cheaper) brand. The contract for making the repairs may be more complex than the contract for the sale and purchase. What you want to do is sell the unit and walk away with your money. You don't want to get into a redecorating contract with your buyer.

We have found that people who are unwilling to invest in their units are not necessarily poor people but rather, frugal people, to be polite. When you prepare to sell your property, you are entering the world of marketing. It doesn't take a marketing major to know that in any selling endeavor, a nice package sells better than a poor presentation, unless you are willing to give it away.

With regard to upgrades, there is a perfectly natural tendency to want to recover monies invested in the property along with the profit on the real estate. Unfortunately, it doesn't always work that way. We were contacted by a client who asked for an appraisal of his property. When we gave him our opinion; he said that it was unacceptable. He then presented us with every receipt he had, indicating to the penny what expenses he incurred with regard to the property, and he wanted to recoup it all. If he put a nail into the wall, he calculated the cost of the nail.

TEACHING POINT: Please recall that at the

..... or competition. But let us suppose that you are in a soft real estate market and there are a number of competing units on the market. You then have your classic situation where supply outweighs demand. If you want to sell, you are going to have to make your unit stand out amongst the others that are now vying for a limited supply of purchasers. Therefore, your purpose now for upgrading is not to raise the price of the unit, but simply to make your apartment more attractive to the limited purchasing pool. In this case, the improvements are going to be sunk costs. Also, you can't expect a buyer to pay for your 20-year-old furniture, which has now fully depreciated.

Sometimes improvements will raise the value of the property. Sometimes they will merely make your property more saleable at the current market value, whatever that is. In a really hot real estate market, it may not be necessary to improve the property and it will sell on the strength of the market alone.

This is—again—where objectivity comes into place.

Being Objective About Upgrading. We stated earlier that you have to be objective about your property. You also have to be objective about the real estate market in your area. In our scenario, there are numerous "like" properties competing on the market. The unit in question has not been upgraded and has also been rented over the years, which means that the furnishings have probably taken their share of wear and tear over the years with each succeeding tenant. The fact that it was professionally decorated ten years ago will have little significance, as styles change over the years. In some locations, 12-by-12-inch marble has been replaced by 24-by-24-inch marble. Large amounts of furniture and lots of bright wallpaper have been replaced in many areas with minimalist furniture and neutral color paint on the walls and no wallpaper.

Here is where the objectivity comes in. You need to look at your property not with the eyes of love, not with the fond memories of good times you had there with spouse or companion, not with recollections of the fun and adventures, or even the aggravations of furnishing the unit for which you now want to exact monetary revenge on the purchasers, but with the cool analytical data and somber and unemotional calculations as to costs and worth in the marketplace. To you, that couch was placed where you and your loved one spent many hours together watching television or reading or whatever and is a priceless artifact that you want to be highly compensated for. But to a buyer, it is an old worn couch that is fully depreciated and will only be an expense to get rid of if he or she were to get stuck with it.

That same objectivity should be employed with the entirety of your unit. Maybe you like living next to the garage, but most buyers don't. You can rationalize that you are close to your car, and it is easy to bring in the groceries. That is all well and good, but it isn't going to replace a twenty-third-floor oceanfront apartment in terms of value in the marketplace.

Do You Have to Upgrade? Before making the decision on what price to list your unit, you should ask yourself if you need to upgrade. We indicated that the market was brisk and there was demand for units in the building, but you have some competition. Which units do you need to be concerned with? You need to be concerned with the units both directly and indirectly competing with you that are upgraded and being shown, although not necessarily sold, with nice furniture. In other words, people who are offering "model" apartments.

The Cost of Upgrading. How much should you spend on upgrading? It depends on a number of factors. If a unit is overimproved—that is, the owner spent more money on the unit than what is generally considered proper for the project—that person will probably not get the money back that was put into the unit, and it might not actually help sell the unit. Depending on the market, you could lose money, and that shouldn't happen in real estate.

For example, let us suppose you purchased a unit in a building with prices averaging around $350,000 in a location where the style is carpeting and rustic furniture. You spend $250,000 on a marble floor, an ultramodern kitchen with stainless steel appliances, and European-style modern furniture. You have overimproved your investment. Buyers may like it but understand that all of the glitz is not in keeping with the location of the

...eveloper competing with you at the same or similar price with newly designed apartments, and is it showing a model apartment? The best advice that we can give is to present a clean, nicely furnished and upgraded apartment to the extent your nearest competition is presenting but without overimproving it. Stay within the standards of the building and the area in general.

Also realize that upgrading a unit may raise the value of the unit or it may just be necessary to compete with your neighbor and will not yield added economic benefit. A lot of that depends on the strength of the market in general and the demand for units in your particular area or building.

Setting Your Price

You have done your research and determined that your nearest competition has an upgraded unit being offered for $620,000. His unit is upgraded and shows well. It is furnished with modern furniture and is very neat. You know the seller and, after a brief conversation with him, determine that his price is flexible or *negotiable,* which means he will probably accept a lower offer.

Now you look objectively at your apartment. The carpets are stained, the furniture is old and beaten up from the years of rentals and general lack of care, and the kitchen appliances are out of date and show the wear. You also notice that the design of the apartment is somewhat dated as well. The rooms are all square, the balcony or "terrace" is smaller than those in newer buildings, and the bathrooms are smaller as well. Newer buildings have larger bathrooms, are not quite so squared in design, and are more open or "European" in design.

Well, you can't change the design of the apartment, or can you? In some cases, it is relatively easy to take down a wall or create a pass-through to give an enclosed kitchen more light and the feeling of openness. Replacing worn and used-looking appliances does not require a great investment either, and if you are a do-it-yourself kind of person, a fresh coat of paint should not break the bank, either. The old adage that you only have one chance to make a first impression is as true for real estate as it is for interviews and sales in general.

You upgrade your appliances, lay some nice wood flooring down, and paint the unit. You replace some of the dated furniture with new, modern-looking items and put some shelving in the master bedroom. You notice that one of the bathroom cabinets is rusty and you replace it, along with the stained bathtub. None of the units have a spa tub, but the local home repair store is offering a special for a few dollars more, so you opt for it. You are amazed at the improvement. Now you are ready to make the vital determination as to listing price.

As indicated previously, your nearest competition is $620,000 but it is two floors above you. Although the rule of thumb for developers is $5,000 per floor, that does not necessarily apply for resales, where the market is not tightly controlled by the developer. Your unit is upgraded similarly to your neighbor, and so you decide to list at $618,000. You correctly figure that any prospect who will look at the other unit will also look at yours for $2,000 less, even though it is on a lower floor. Since you know that your competition is flexible and the last price to sell was $580,000, you, too, will listen to offers in that price range.

You also decide to sell the unit unfurnished but will be willing to add it into the price as a negotiating tool. Thus, if the prospective purchaser makes you an offer close to your asking price but wants the furniture as part of the deal, you are willing to accept it and give the furniture.

Marketing Your Property

Now that you have decided on a price, do you list with a broker or try to sell it yourself and save the commission? We always recommend that you employ professional people to get professional results. For our purposes, we will use the term *broker* to describe any person involved in the sale of real estate, even though there may be technical differences between brokers and sales agents, depending on state licensing laws. In most cases, a broker is the head of the office, while the agents are those who work for the broker. As in all professions, some professionals are better than others, and it takes research and a bit of common sense to choose the right brokers.

Choosing a Broker

..., ~. a ~..........a. lawyer from one who does wills and trusts for a living. Other factors include the location of the broker, experience as a broker or agent, the amount of sales made in your neighborhood, and the amount of listings the brokerage firm has in your area and the type of advertising done by the firm.

Location of the broker is self-explanatory. You obviously want a broker who is close to your unit and is available to show it during normal business hours, sometimes on short notice. There are numerous brokers and listings in the marketplace, and if the broker isn't available until "next Thursday" to show your apartment, the prospect may cool or you may lose the deal to some other broker who is ready, willing, and able to show listings.

Broker experience is also pretty much self-explanatory. The more experience in condominium-related sales, the more likely that the broker will be successful. If you are having surgery, who would you rather have operate on you—a doctor with 2 years of experience who operated on a handful of patients, or a doctor with 15 years of experience who has operated on thousands of patients? In professional situations, results are what count. Your broker may be the nicest person or try very hard, but if he or she doesn't sell your property, you are not going to be happy.

Not so obvious is the amount of listings the broker in your area has that are similar to your apartment. This is two-edged sword. On one hand, it is indicative of the success of a broker who commands the majority of the listings in an area as the "go to" person to get your apartment sold. On the other hand, if a broker has too many competing listings, it may lessen the chances of yours being sold. In most cases, the issue is resolved by the broker's record of sales in the particular building or area, and that should be your main determining factor. Sometimes, a broker who has a great number of listings is merely a broker skilled at obtaining listings. Sooner or later some will sell through no particular device of the broker, and that gives a false indication of the skill of the broker at selling rather than just obtaining the listings for sale.

Advertising is another area that is deceptive in determining whether a broker is skilled at sales or not. Some brokerage firms offer extensive advertising in newspapers and magazines that impresses sellers so they list with that brokerage firm. However, in some cases, the fancy advertising may be designed to bring in business rather than to actually get sales results. For example, in areas where there is a multiple listing service (a computerized databank consulted by brokers on behalf of buyers looking for property), this may be the most effective method of advertising. In areas that don't have this service and rely solely on the independent advertising of the agency, then how a broker markets the property becomes relevant.

As already indicated, we believe that you should hire professionals to do a professional job. Having said that, what are the bottom-line criteria for selecting a broker to market your property, and what are the various types of agreements you will be asked to sign in the hiring process? After this discussion, we will also offer some tips for those who insist on doing it themselves.

Listing Agreements

Let us assume that you have located a local broker with vast experience in the location and type of property that you are marketing. Generally, there are three types of contracts, or *listing agreements,* standard in the industry:

1. An *exclusive right of sale listing agreement* is a *bilateral* contract between you and the broker. It gives the broker the sole or "exclusive" right to market your property. If you sell it yourself or through another broker, you will be responsible for paying your broker his or her full commission.

Most sellers resist this type of agreement because they think it is too restrictive. They believe that the more brokers there are working for them, the greater the chance of selling the apartment, and most believe or hope that they can ultimately do it themselves and save the commission. Whether or not this theory is correct depends on systems employed by the broker to sell the property. In areas that have a multiple listing service through their local or regional realtor association, an exclusive listing right of sale agreement is usually the best and sellers should not resist signing. In areas that do not have such a marketing system, you should resist signing such an agreement with the broker. Before we explain this in detail, we should discuss the other types of agreements you may be offered.

2. An *open listing* simply means that anyone is free to sell the property, but if the broker with an open listing sells it, that broker would get the stipulated commission. It is simply an agreement between you and your broker to memorialize how much this particular broker will charge if

───── to effectuate the sale.

As already stated, which type of contract you select depends on the marketing system in the area where your property is located. For example, in an area that has an extensive multiple listing service where brokers list their properties for other brokers to see, you are well advised to sign an exclusive listing agreement. The reason for this is broker cooperation. In areas where there is a Realtor listing service, cooperation between the brokers is encouraged and all area brokers have the same opportunity to share the information and bring their clients to see the properties. You pay your broker the commission under the terms of your listing agreement and the broker splits with the cooperating broker. It is the same as having hundreds or thousands of brokers working for you at the same time, and in our opinion, it is the single most effective method of marketing a property. It is far more effective than the seller offering the property to a few brokers under an open listing agreement, where cooperation between brokers is not encouraged because there is little to protect them if they attempt to market the property.

However, what if your property is located in an area where there is no Realtor service? Well, then there is no incentive to hire a single broker. In those areas, each broker works on his or her own to sell the property and competes rather than cooperates with other brokers. In those cases, you would want maximum competition between the brokers, and the best way to achieve a successful sale is through open listings rather than to rely on one broker to advertise on his or her own.

Selling Without a Broker

When you employ a broker in the U.S. or Latin America, the broker generally absorbs the cost of the advertising. What happens if you are a do-it-yourself person and you want to market the property on your own? Some of the following tips will be good advice for you if you act on your own.

Advertising. The first thing you will want to do is advertise the property. Many people now have their own web sites, but unless you have a professional service that ensures that your site will be on the first ten or so "hits" on the major search engines such as Yahoo!, AOL, or Google, the odds that anyone will see your site (other than your friends) is not very good. There are a number of real estate search engines that will list your property for a small fee. In Europe, the Internet is a major factor in real estate marketing because there are no common Realtor services and it is a crucial part of their advertising—in some cases, supplanting newspaper ads. In the United States, we would argue that this is not yet the case. For sales in the United States, it is our opinion that the newspaper is still the primary source for advertising real estate, although the Internet should not be ignored. The next question is, what is the content of a good solid advertisement?

Placing an ad in the newspaper can be expensive. Most charge by the word or by the line. There are extra charges for highlighting your ad with little stars or hearts or in bold text. We recommend paying the extra charges because there are going to be numerous ads, and you want the readers to see yours. The next thing you want to do is be specific and brief. Here is an example of a good solid ad:

APARTMENT FOR SALE
2 BD/2.5 BTH
HIGH FLR, VIEW OF PARK,
UNIVERSAL CONDOMINIUM
UNFRNSHD
$350,000
Call Ted at 555-555-5555

Let's analyze the advertisement. With a limited amount of space and cost, you have told prospective purchasers that your unit has two bedrooms, two and a half baths, and is on a high floor with a view of the park. You have given the name of the condominium and the fact that you will sell unfurnished. You have also given the price and contact number. This should be enough information to garner inquiries from people who are looking for your type of unit.

Some sellers as well as agents don't give the price of the unit. The thinking is that you get as many calls as possible and so on, line is

Being Available for Potential Buyers. When selling property either through a broker or on your own, one of the key factors is to have the property available for showing. If you work during the week and you can only show on weekends that may limit your ability to sell the unit. If you don't want to be bothered showing in the evening, that may be a problem as well. The fact is, the more available your unit is for showing, the greater the chance for a quicker sale.

The same applies for answering the phone. If you supply a phone number, make sure there is someone who will be available to answer the call. You can limit the hours to times you will be available, but every limitation you place in your ad limits the potential buyers for your unit.

One last reminder: It is unfortunate, but we live in a dangerous world and you are advertising in it. Perfect strangers will be coming to your home. If you are alone when you are showing, have a friend come with you. It may sound paranoid, but be safe.

Keeping Your Unit Ready to Show. If you are living in the property, make sure your unit is *show ready* at all times. Don't leave your dirty underwear or towels all over the place. Be sure the bed is made and the place is clean and bright and uncluttered.

How many model apartments have you visited where the bed was unmade and unmentionables were hanging over the bathroom shower and the dishes were piled up in the sink? We have stressed throughout this book that when you buy or sell real estate, you are in business. It is business when you market your own personal residence, and you must be professional, so sales rules apply if you want to make the sale efficiently and maximize your price.

Closing the Sale

Now we reach the big finish, the reason for this whole process from the time you bought until now, the actual sale. There have been responses to your ad, and one of the prospects wants to make an offer. What do you do? The prospect, now known in the parlance of real estate as the *offeror,* needs to make that offer in writing with a deposit. That requires a contract.

Real estate form contracts may be purchased at a local office supply store, but you are better disposed to have an attorney prepare one for you, or get a contract from the local board of Realtors. Form contracts may not address the unique aspects of your sale or the particularities of state law, even if the writers of the form claim they are good in all fifty states. Many people tend to minimize the importance of a solid contract until something goes wrong. Then all parties refer to the contract, and if it is incomplete, it can be costly in both the possible collapse of the sale and further attorney's fees.

Earlier in this book, we reviewed the portions of the contract from the buyer's side, so you should be familiar with them. However, although this is a do-it-yourself book and it is possible and legal to write your own contract, it is not advisable. There is simply no substitute for a lawyer at this point in the transaction. Even real estate professionals who are authorized to prepare contracts often get it wrong when they have to put in additional clauses that are not incorporated in the preprinted forms. Most contracts we have reviewed that have been written by sellers or buyers are woefully incomplete. Further, even if you get it right, there are other issues that need to be dealt with, such as title search, insurance, and recording of documents.

In Chapter 7, we left off our discussion with the HUD statement and touched on the issue of title insurance and recording of documents. As indicated earlier, when you as the seller provide a deed, theoretically you are guaranteeing that you have good title to the property (unless it is a quit-claim deed). You are offering assurance that in fact you own what you are selling. In reality, when sellers get their money, they are rarely heard from again.

Proof of Title

Most contracts call for the seller to provide some proof of title ownership, and it is then incumbent upon the buyer to make sure that the seller is providing good title to the property. Unless you are versed in the searching of titles and recording of deeds and mortgages and numerous other types of liens that can encumber or cloud a title, you will need to employ a title company and purchase title insurance. Who pays for this is always negotiable, but the general standard in the United States is that it is the seller who

_..._ _. ._ _... y_ _ears, there_

should be a continuous history of the transactions regarding that particular piece of property.

Fortunately, most condominiums and cooperatives only date back several years rather than hundreds of years, and with computer technology it is relatively easy to check whether there are any problems with the title. A title examiner would be looking for anything that caused the title on the property to be at fault. It could be anything from a *mechanic's lien*, a lien that some repairperson filed against the property because he or she wasn't paid by a previous owner, to some fraudulent activity, such as the property being sold twice to different buyers. The examiner is looking for a clear or clean title—that is, a title with no *encumbrances* upon it such as the aforementioned mechanic's lien.

If this sounds a bit scary and complicated, it is. Not only do you want to make sure that you have clear title, but you also want to make sure your new title is correctly recorded so that you are protected as well. Even where the seller is a legitimate and honest person, as in most cases, and will not try and resell the property a second time, proper recording is still crucial because at the time you as the new buyer want to sell the property, you will need to show the same unbroken chain of title that you demanded when you purchased the property.

At the Closing

Let's review the basic documents you will need to prepare for the closing. As the seller, you will need a copy of the contract and your evidence of good title and an estoppel letter. An *estoppel letter* is a letter, usually provided by the condominium association or cooperative association, which states that you have paid your maintenance and any special assessments to date. That is pretty much it for the seller.

The buyer has a bit more work to do. The buyer needs to receive the evidence of title from the seller and have the title examined and updated to make sure the seller may sell the property free and clear of any encumbrances. The buyer also needs to have financing in order, as discussed in Chapter 8. When the research and documents are prepared, a closing is set up.

At the *closing,* there will be a variety of players. The cast of characters varies, depending on how the transaction was handled. Assuming every type of professional was employed, there will be an attorney for the seller (or developer), who will act as the closing agent, or there could be a separate title service, which may be representing the bank as well and handling the transaction for both parties. The respective brokers for the buyer and seller will probably be present to answer any questions about the transaction and, more importantly, to receive their commission checks.

Once the participants are seated, the closing process will begin. The following describes the standard closing process:

1. The seller will sign the deed. If there is personal property involved, the seller might sign a bill of sale for such items as the refrigerator, oven, and other appliances.

2. The closing agent will then go over the HUD or settlement statement with you and take any questions regarding the calculations. The settlement agent generally does not represent either party and will not intervene in controversies between the parties. His or her only job is to defend the settlement statement. Once you are satisfied with your portion of the settlement statement, the closing agent will then turn to the buyer.

3. If there is a mortgage involved, the buyer will begin the process of signing the mortgage papers.

4. The closing agent will also go over the settlement statement with the buyer as well.

5. The buyer should then have checks that match the amounts on the settlement statement that are due and owing to you as the seller. Once the checks are received, the settlement agent distributes the funds to the various parties, including the brokers, if any.

6. At the end of the closing, the buyer should have a warranty deed, a settlement statement, any assignments such as parking or storage spaces and bill of sale for personal property and the title insurance policy.

TAXES

Not to end on a bad note, but a word or two must be said concerning taxes. There are new federal laws that apply to the sale of real estate, and many people—even professionals—are confused as to what the current state of the law is. As this book is being written, investment property, that is, property that is not your principal residence, is subject to a capital gains tax of up to 15 percent of the profits.

U.S. citizens who occupy their homes as primary residences for two years are no longer subject to capital gains. This exemption may be used an unlimited number of times, as long as they purchase and reside in the properties as their primary residence for at least a two-year period.

Foreign investors may be subject to a variety of tax laws, including the Foreign Investors Real Property Tax Act (FIRPTA). There are several tests that determine if you are a U.S. resident or a foreign investor for tax purposes. Non-U.S. citizens who own property in the United States should contact an attorney regarding these issues.

CONCLUSION

Real estate in the form of land holdings has historically been the symbol of wealth for the privileged aristocratic few. Today, that is no longer the case. Almost everyone can acquire some sort of real estate holding. Condominiums, cooperatives, townhouses, hotel-condominiums, and timeshares are but a few of the wide variety of real estate opportunities available to those willing to make the investment. It's fun and potentially very profitable. So good luck, and enjoy the world of real estate.

The following quiz is based on the material in this book to see if you have grasped the principles that we have been discussing. I will give you the answers with explanations at the end of this section, but try to answer the questions yourself before skipping ahead.

CONDOS, CO-OPS, AND TOWNHOUSES

1. You have purchased an apartment in a building containing 50 units. You have received a deed and set of condominium documents. You have purchased a _____.
   a. Timeshare
   b. Condominium
   c. Hotel-condominium
   d. All of the above

2. You have purchased an apartment in a building containing 150 units. You are assigned your apartment by the board of directors of the building. You have purchased a _____.
   a. Timeshare
   b. Condominium
   c. Townhouse
   d. Cooperative

3. Which of the following *does not* represent an investment in real estate?
   a. Timeshare
   b. Cooperative
   c. Hotel-condominium
   d. b and c.

4. One reason why timeshares did not reach their full potential as a real estate investment was:
   a. It was a terrible idea.
   b. It was a good idea but poorly implemented.
   c. It was not an investment in real estate.
   d. None of the above.

5. You have purchased a condominium. The NBA playoffs are on and you want to see them via satellite television. You call the satellite company, and they install the dish on the outer wall of the building. They explain that this is the only place where you can get proper reception. The day before the first game, you get a call from the building manager, who explains that the rules of the association do not allow satellite dishes to be attached to the building and orders you to take down the dish. What should you do?
   a. Tell the manager to #@★&̂%.
   b. *Politely* explain that this is a condominium, you are an owner, and you have every right to have a satellite dish.
   c. Remove the satellite dish and get cable.
   d. All of the above are correct.

6. Those portions of a condominium that are shared by all the members are known as _____.
   a. Community property
   b. Community elements
   c. Common elements
   d. Recreation leases

7. Condominiums, cooperatives, timeshares, and hotel-condominiums all have the following in common:
   a. They are investments in real estate.
   b. They are governed by homeowners associations.
   c. When purchased, you receive a deed to your property.
   d. All of the above.

8. For which purchase will you likely receive two sets of condominium documents?
   a. Timeshare
   b. Hotel-condominium

...ming can be done. Based on these facts, the type of property you were seeking to purchase was probably a _____.
   a. Cooperative
   b. Hotel-condominium
   c. Condominium
   d. None of the above, because a board of directors cannot reject you if you are willing to pay the price.

10. The landscaping around the condominium is not looking too good. You should:
   a. Get together with your neighbors and hold a gardening party.
   b. Forget about it; it makes no difference.
   c. Complain to the building manager or the board of directors.
   d. Complain only if you are planning to sell your property, because if the building appears unkept, it could negatively affect your sales price.

11. You want to make a real estate investment but are used to living in a large apartment complex. Which should you most likely choose?
   a. Townhouse
   b. Condominium
   c. Cooperative
   d. Hotel-condominium

12. You don't want to purchase a private house but do want a private garage, a small yard or deck, and a swimming pool. You most likely would prefer:
   a. A townhouse
   b. A timeshare

     c. A hotel-condominum

     d. A condominium

13. You want to live in a large complex with nice amenities, but you can't afford to pay high condominium prices. You may wish to look for _____.

     a. A townhouse

     b. A hotel-condominum

     c. A timeshare

     d. A cooperative

14. You take the same two-week vacation each year at the same resort. You want to make a small real estate investment in a vacation property and you would also like to travel. Which should you look at?

     a. Timeshare

     b. Hotel-condominum

     c. Townhouse

     d. A good travel agent

15. You don't want a private house but you have heard horror stories about boards of directors. You want to make a purchase in real estate for you and your family to live in. You should probably look at:

     a. A townhouse

     b. A hotel-condominum

     c. Timeshare

     d. None of the above

16. You want to invest in real estate. You don't particularly care what type of real estate category it falls under, as long as it comes with a swimming pool, tennis court, and gymnasium, which are things you really value. You should look at:

     a. A townhouse

     b. A condominium

     c. A cooperative

     d. Any type of residential community association

17. You have a spouse, three spirited kids, and two very large dogs. On Sundays, you love to invite family and friends and have a barbeque. You don't want a private house. Your best bet for a real estate investment would be:

     a. A hotel-condominum

b. A timeshare
c. A condominium
d. A townhouse

18. V_{--} 1

19. You hate rules and regulations and consider yourself an individualist and a renegade. You own a huge truck with a hitch for towing a boat, which you use seasonally and store in your garage the rest of the year. You often repair vintage cars in your garage ramp and yard. You also own several motorcycles—none of which have mufflers, because you feel it insults the free integrity of the engine. To you, noise is beautiful. Which should you purchase?
a. Timeshare
b. Condominium
c. Townhouse
d. None of the above

Searching for the Right Property

20. In determining if a real estate investment is suitable, one should always consider:
a. Specific location of the investment
b. The general area as a whole
c. The history of the area
d. All of the above

21. The following factors are all relevant to the area in which a real estate investment is located except:
a. Proximity to schools
b. History of the area
c. Public transportation
d. Proximity to your work

22. Why are perceptions of an area where a real estate investment is located important?
    a. They may be indicative of the potential appreciation of the investment.
    b. They may indicate ease of resale of the property.
    c. They provide a history of the area where the investment is located.
    d. All of the above.

23. Questions you should ask to gain a perception of the area include:
    a. Was the area previously commercial or residential?
    b. Is the area considered safe to live in?
    c. What type of people live in the neighborhood?
    d. a and b but not c.

24. All of the following are economic factors that you should consider in a condominium real estate investment except:
    a. Building costs
    b. Asking price of the condominium
    c. Interest rates on a mortgage for the property
    d. You should consider all three.

25. Your broker offers you an oceanfront condominium in south Florida and tells you that you should buy it because "location, location, location says it all." The apartment is indeed beautiful, and you really want to buy it. You should do the following:
    a. Put down a deposit immediately before someone else grabs it.
    b. Buy it because an oceanfront condominium is the ultimate location and you can't lose. The broker is right in this case.
    c. Do all of the research on the area, perceptions, and economics (A.P.E.), just as you would any other real estate investment.
    d. Buy it only if you can get a good mortgage.

26. You are in the market for a second home to use for vacations. You find a lovely condominium in a new lakeside community that is under construction. The resort will have access to golf, a beautiful lake, horseback riding, tennis, and a restaurant, although the golf course has not been constructed yet and the tennis courts are not completed. The nearest airport is around an hour by car, and the closest town is 30 minutes by car. You love it. You should:
    a. Plunk down a deposit without further hesitation.

  b. Check to see if there are any other similar communities in that area.
  c. Research the developers of the community.
  d. b and c but not a

use, and plans for condominium construction are in the works, although none have been constructed as yet. The best course of action is to:

  a. Make the purchase in accordance with the laws governing co-operative purchases because the price is right and the apartment has a good floor plan.
  b. Make the purchase because the floor plan is good and the price is right, but understand that the area is in a state of flux and there is no guarantee that it will develop in accordance with plans. This could have an adverse effect on the value of your purchase.
  c. Walk away from the deal; it is too risky.
  d. Before making a decision, check with the local planning commission to see if any developers have put in for zoning changes or construction permits, see what other residents of the city think about living in this area, and check if the banks are willing to finance a loan on this particular piece of property. Then make the decision.

28. You have a spouse and two children and need to move to a larger home. You and your spouse have to decide whether to purchase a detached house, townhouse, or condominium. You find a townhouse in a community very close to good schools, shopping, and transportation, but it would require you spend an extra half hour in traffic commuting to work. Your spouse will, however, be closer to work. The community is growing, and there is residential property being constructed everywhere you turn. The broker tells you that this is a sign of a vibrant, growing community with great in-

vestment potential. "It's like having money in the bank," says the broker. You should:

a. Make the purchase, because your children are of the utmost concern and good schools are always an overriding factor.

b. Don't make the purchase because all of the new construction may be signs of a vibrant community but the developers may be creating too much supply, which may translate into increased competition for you should you decide to sell you townhouse in the future, which in turn may cause its value to drop.

c. As long as your spouse is closer to his or her work, making the purchase is the unselfish thing that a good spouse does, provided your spouse earns more than you do.

d. Consider making the purchase, but try to determine the factors with regard to your townhouse or community that makes it more desirable than the multitude of other similar projects in the surrounding area.

29. You are considering a second home as a real estate investment. However, you travel a great deal and will probably not use the property very much. After due consideration, you select a hotel-condominium for your investment. The area is excellent for that style of investment, and everyone loves to vacation at that particular resort. Occupancy is at 80 percent to 95 percent most of the year due to a robust convention trade in addition to the seasonal tourists. Everything looks good until you go to the bank. For some reason, the local banks are not financing the project but won't give you any specific information as to the reason. The broker tells you not to worry—he says it is just that local banks are not used to hotel-condominiums as a concept but that he can arrange financing for you. What should you do?

a. Find out why local area banks won't finance the project.

b. Don't bother investigating, just run away from this deal and this broker.

c. Take the broker's financing if it is competitive and make the investment because the occupancy rate indicates that it is a good investment.

d. Never invest in a hotel-condominium unless it is 100 percent occupied at least three quarters of the year.

30. You can't decide whether to buy a condominium or a townhouse. In the area you are looking at, the townhouses are cheaper but

appreciate less because there are so many of them and more are being built. The bank says you can qualify for both and the rates are better for the townhouse. What should you do?

a. Definitely buy the townhouse

....idents to see how they perceive the area.

b. Look at the projected neighborhood amenities such as transportation, shopping, entertainment, and parking and security.

c. Try to calculate the risk versus the possible return of such an investment.

d. All of the above.

BUYING FROM A DEVELOPER

32. When purchasing directly from a developer, which of the following is not true?

a. Purchasing from a developer requires the same research as any other purchase of real estate.

b. Purchasing from a developer guarantees the property will appreciate.

c. Purchasers should always check to see what their rescission rights are.

d. Real estate brokers may be a valuable source of aid in purchasing from a developer.

33. When considering a purchase directly from a developer, the purchaser should be prepared to:

a. Listen carefully to the developer's salesperson.

b. View the model unit if there is one available.

c. Have a prepared list of questions.

d. All of the above.

34. One of the benefits of buying directly from a developer is:

a. You are guaranteed an apartment that will appreciate in value.

     b. You are guaranteed that the developer will finish the project to the highest standards.

     c. You will get new appliances.

     d. You will always get the best deal.

35. Using a real estate broker to purchase from a developer:

     a. Is totally unnecessary since the developer has all the information you need.

     b. Will jeopardize the deal because developers don't like real estate brokers.

     c. May help you because real estate brokers may possess superior information about developments and developers.

     d. Will hinder the deal because you can negotiate a better deal without the broker because the developer won't have to pay a commission to the broker.

36. All of the following represent a risk when purchasing from a developer except:

     a. The developer may not finish the project.

     b. The project will be completed but not be as nice as represented at the sales office.

     c. The project will not appreciate as fast as the salesperson predicts.

     d. All of the above represent risks of a purchase directly from the developer.

37. Questions you should ask the developer's sales agent should not include:

     a. How many people do they estimate will actually reside full time in the building?

     b. What is included by the developer in the unit?

     c. How many members of a certain religion will live in the building?

     d. Which bank is financing the project?

38. When a developer advertises that its project is 80 percent sold, it may mean that:

     a. The developer is creating a sense of urgency.

     b. 80 percent of the inventory is indeed sold.

     c. 80 percent of the released inventory is sold but there is more inventory not yet released.

     d. All of the above.

39. All of the following are true about sales brochures except:
    a. They will tell you something about the developer.
    b. They will give you information about the project.
    c. They are a substitute for good research

... when considering purchasing a project from a developer, you should consult all of the following except:
    a. Local area brokers.
    b. Local residents.
    c. Uncle Herb and Aunt Ida, who are really nice, but are not experts in real estate
    d. Local bankers.

BUYING A RESALE

42. One advantage of buying a resale rather than a new property from a developer is:
    a. You don't have to do any research.
    b. You see what you are getting.
    c. It is a better deal to buy a resale.
    d. You have less negotiating power when buying a resale.

43. You find a condominium you like, and the local real estate broker tells you that three others like yours have sold for $100,000, $125,000, and $110,000. You should make an offer of:
    a. $85,000
    b. $75,000
    c. $125,000
    d. Impossible to tell; you don't have enough information.

44. You find a condominium you like. The local real estate broker tells you that three others like yours have sold for $100,000, $110,000, and $125,000 within the last six months. There are two others in the building like yours for sale at $185,000 and $190,000 and it is

a seller's market. The unit you want is listed at $187,500. What should you offer?
a. $75,000
b. $125,000
c. $165,000
d. $200,000

45. The same facts as questions #44, except that you are advised that the market has changed to a buyer's market and there is more property coming on the market. What should you offer?
a. $75,000
b. $125,000
c. $165,000
d. $200,000

46. The contract for a pre-owned home should include
a. The offer to buy.
b. Who pays for closing costs.
c. If there is any rescission period.
d. All of the above.

47. When relocating from a large private house to a condominum, you should consider everything but
a. How you are going to get your furniture to fit.
b. The price of the purchase.
c. The location of the unit.
d. The condominium documents.

48. When purchasing a resale, what course should you take?
a. Engage the services of a qualified broker because the broker can provide you with valuable information concerning your purchase.
b. You should never engage a broker because he or she always represents the seller.
c. Hire the broker, but pay the commission yourself.
d. Never hire a broker because you can negotiate a better deal without one.

49. Erik and Erika engage a real estate broker to help them find a condominium. The broker shows them several properties and they select one from the broker's listing inventory. Erik and Erika should:

a. Engage another broker because this broker has a conflict of interest with the owner of the property who gave him the listing.

b. Use the broker because his fiduciary relationship switches from the seller to the buyer

a. Buy it solely on the basis of the fact that it is a good deal.

b. Pass on the purchase because they don't like it.

c. Make a low-ball offer and if it is accepted, buy it.

d. Pass on the purchase and look for a property they both like.

PAPERWORK

51. Where will the basic blueprint for a real estate transaction involving the sale and purchase of a condominium be found?
    a. The condominium documents
    b. The HUD statement
    c. The contract
    d. The condominium's storage area, provided it is a limited common element

52. For a contract to be binding it must contain the following elements:
    a. Offer and acceptance
    b. The name of the buyer and seller
    c. The name of the buyer and the time of the closing
    d. Offer, acceptance, consideration, and a definite end date

53. John and Mary enter into a contract to sell their condominium to Paul and Sammy. What is this called?
    a. A condominium contract
    b. A bilateral contract
    c. A unilateral contract
    d. A divorce proceeding

54. In terms of real estate contracts, which of the following is a true statement?
    a. A person who purchases from a developer has more bargaining power in terms of structuring a contract.
    b. A purchaser of a resale unit has more bargaining power in terms of structuring a contract.
    c. A resale contract is considered a contract of adhesion.
    d. Oral real estate contracts are generally enforceable under the statute of frauds.

55. You are considering purchasing a unit in a hotel-condominium but want to know your rights with regard to the amenities offered. Who or what should you consult?
    a. The condominium documents
    b. Your attorney
    c. Your real estate broker
    d. The condominium association board of directors

56. According to the condominium documents, you have the exclusive right to use a storage bin that is assigned to your unit, but you do not own it. This storage bin is probably
    a. Damp and smelly, and not someplace you should store your valuables.
    b. A common element.
    c. A bilateral agreement between you and the association.
    d. A limited common element.

57. According to the rules and regulations of the association, the swimming pool of the condominium is only open until 7:00 P.M. Which is correct?
    a. This is not a valid rule and you can swim whenever you want.
    b. This is a valid rule that is enforceable under the condominium documents.
    c. Because use of a common element can't be governed by the association, this is an invalid rule.
    d. In a free society, you have an inalienable right to swim, so this rule is not valid.

58. The HUD statement does all of the following except:
    a. State the amount of money the buyer will pay and the seller will receive for the property.

    b. Reflect prorated sums as of the date of the closing or as stipulated in the contract.

    c. List recording and other fees associated with the transaction.

    d. Convey title to the ~~property~~

~~stipulates that~~ time is of the essence"?

    a. It means that either the buyer or the seller is a senior citizen.

    b. There is no hurry on either party's side and the contract may continue until both sides are ready to close.

    c. Both sides must strictly adhere to the time constraints of the contract or risk default.

    d. None of the above.

FINANCING

61. The first place you should go when investigating a loan for real estate is _____.

    a. Your local banker

    b. Your mortgage banker

    c. Your mortgage broker

    d. Grandma

62. Which of the following is not a lending institution?

    a. Mortgage banker

    b. Mortgage broker

    c. Bank

    d. All of the above are lending institutions.

63. The person who generally has the final approval for your loan is known as the _____.

    a. Undertaker

    b. The branch manager of the bank

    c. Underwriter

    d. Underwear salesman

64. Before you choose a loan package you should:

    a. Check various lending institutions.

    b. Take the lowest interest rate regardless of the other terms and conditions.

    c. Make sure the entire package is right for you.

    d. Do whatever your lending institution advises.

65. What factors might affect the rate of interest on your mortgage?

    a. Your credit score

    b. The type of property you are buying

    c. The value of the property you are buying

    d. All of the above

66. If there is a fee for paying off the loan early, this is known as a _____.

    a. Foreclosure

    b. Prepayment penalty

    c. Postpayment penalty

    d. Commission

67. Banks may request the following information when processing a loan:

    a. Your social security number

    b. Three years of tax returns

    c. Three months of bank statements

    d. All of the above

68. When you pay the lending institution a sum of money in advance to lower the interest rate, it is known as _____.

    a. Points

    b. Buydown

    c. Bribe

    d. Payoff

69. What should happen prior to the closing of your property?

    a. You should have received and reviewed all of the loan documentation including the HUD closing statement.

    b. You should make sure that the bank is ready to close on the date stipulated in the contract.

c. You should verify that terms and conditions of the loan are what you agreed to.

d. All of the above.

70. You purchased a condominium for $250,000

........CONDO LIVING

71. When moving into a condominium, you should:

a. Consult with the manager as to the move-in rules.

b. Make sure the freight elevator is reserved for your movers.

c. Pay any move-in deposits required.

d. All of the above.

72. You are moving into a newly constructed condominium and you are preparing to put tile and carpeting in your unit. What should you do?

a. Hire contractors and place the floor as you see fit because it is being done in the interior of your unit.

b. Consult the condominium documents as to any soundproofing or other requirements associated with the placing of flooring.

c. Only use carpeting because walking on tile or marble can disturb your neighbors.

d. Whatever you want; soundproofing cannot be regulated by the condominium documents.

73. You hire a contractor to do some electrical work in your unit. He tells you that you must first obtain a permit from the city and that you should go to the city and get the permit in your name. What should you do?

a. Go to the city and obtain the permit in your name.

b. Go to the city and obtain the permit in your name but also put the contractor's name down.

c. Tell the contractor to go to the city and obtain a permit in his name alone.

d. Let your brother-in-law do the repairs, even though he is a butcher by trade.

74. You purchase a condominium resale from another owner. You hire a contractor to install a new sink, commode, and bathtub. The contractor tells you he needs a permit from the city. What should you do?

   a. Hire another contractor.
   b. Tell him he's wrong because the bathtub, commode, and sink are located on private property, not common or limited common elements.
   c. Tell the contractor that plumbing is not subject to permits.
   d. Let the contractor file the permit.

75. Your upstairs neighbor leaves the bathtub running while preparing dinner. Meanwhile, the doorbell rings and while answering it, the neighbor doesn't notice the bathtub overflowing and the dinner burning, which sets off the automatic sprinkler system in the building. Your apartment is flooded due to the overflowing bathtub and the common-element hallway is flooded from the sprinkler system.

   a. The building's liability insurance will cover all the damages.
   b. The building's insurance will cover the hallway damage but not the damage to your unit.
   c. The upstairs neighbor is liable to the building but not to you.
   d. Your personal homeowners insurance will cover the flooding in your apartment and the hallway.

76. It is Sunday afternoon in the summer—the temperature is 100 degrees in the shade. Suddenly, your air conditioning fails. What should you do?

   a. Call the building's manager, who will promptly fix it.
   b. Call your appliance repair insurance carrier if you have a policy, or else call an emergency repair service.
   c. Call the insurance agent who sold you your homeowners policy.
   d. Sweat it out; it is a good opportunity to lose some extra weight.

77. You just bought a satellite dish that can give you 10,000 channels of sports from around the globe. The installer places it on the outside center of the building between your terrace and your neighbor's terrace. Your neighbor complains to the association board of

directors, who promptly order you to take the dish down. What is the *best* response?

a. Invite the board to watch the Latvian Ice Wrestling Championships with you because they don't have the ~~~~ ~~

~~~~ ~~~ ~~~~~~~~ outside of your terrace boundaries, you are probably okay.

78. Your next-door neighbor is a drummer with a local rock band. He practices all day long and has jam sessions with other groups all night long. The local noise ordinance states, "There shall be no excessive noise after 11:00 P.M. and before 9:00 A.M." The police refuse to respond prior to 11:00 P.M., citing the noise ordinance. What is your best course of action?
    a. You are stuck because the police refuse to respond.
    b. Buy a guitar and try to join the band.
    c. Consult the manager; if that fails, consult an attorney because this type of noise may be both excessive and unreasonable.
    d. You can only enforce noise restrictions after 11:00 P.M. Otherwise, your neighbor has a right to play his music.

79. You are frustrated with all the rules and regulations of the association. What should you do?
    a. Move to a house.
    b. Petition the board to ease restrictions.
    c. Protest the rules by disobeying them.
    d. Make up your own rules.

80. You bring a beer to the swimming pool in a glass rather than a paper cup. The rules specifically state that all beverages consumed at or about the pool area must be in paper cups. The condo commando spots you and gives you a ten-minute lecture on the rules of the association. What should you do?
    a. Tell this person to take a hike and walk away.
    b. Listen politely and walk away.

c. Complain to the manager.

d. None of the above.

SELLING

81. At the closing table, you should expect to see all of the following except:

a. The buyer's attorney

b. The seller's attorney

c. The closing agent

d. Your local banker who got you the loan

82. You are preparing to sell your unit, which has not been decorated or upgraded for ten years. What should you do?

a. Spend whatever it takes to make the unit into the best apartment on the market.

b. Spend as much as it takes to make the unit competitive with similar units on the market.

c. Not spend a dime on the unit because the buyer will fix it to his or her own taste.

d. Only repair appliances that aren't properly functioning.

83. When pricing a unit for sale, you should:

a. Consult with a local broker.

b. Consult with your brother-in-law who owns a similar unit in another state.

c. Consult with your neighbors.

d. None of the above.

84. Selling a contract on an apartment prior to closing is referred to as _____.

a. Tossing

b. Turning

c. Flipping

d. Churning

85. When listing a unit with a broker, you should:

a. Always sign an exclusive right of sale agreement.

b. Never sign an exclusive right of sale agreement.

c. Possibly sign an exclusive right of sale agreement, depending on whether there is a multiple listing system in your area.

      d. Never use a broker unless there is a multiple listing service in the area.

86. Where real estate is sold, a capital gains tax may be assessed on:
    a. Foreign investors.

    d. b and c

88. You place an ad in the newspaper for the sale of your apartment. The ad should contain the following except:
    a. The price.
    b. The name of the building.
    c. Brief description of the view or other distinctive selling point.
    d. Terms and conditions of the contract.

89. To insure a smooth closing, a buyer should:
    a. Review the settlement statement prior to the closing.
    b. Make sure his or her bank is ready with the money and paperwork prior to the closing.
    c. Bring up any unresolved issues at the closing table.
    d. a and b.

90. Buyers should walk away from a real estate closing with the following documents:
    a. Warranty deed, bill of sale, title insurance, settlement statement, keys to the property
    b. Warranty deed, bill of sale, broker's commission check, settlement statement
    c. Warranty deed, bill of sale, settlement agreement, seller's check for the proceeds
    d. Warranty deed, bill of sale, title insurance, two sets of car keys

ANSWERS

   1. The correct answer is (d). Condominiums, timeshares, and hotel-condominiums represent purchases of condominium style real es-

tate and consequently are conveyed to the purchaser by deed. In addition, the basic framework for each of these condominium investments, along with the rules and regulations that the owners must follow, are contained in the condominium documents.

2. The correct answer is (d). A cooperative is not, strictly speaking, a purchase of real property, but rather, a purchase of shares in a corporate entity whose asset is the apartment building. You, the purchaser, are then assigned your unit.

3. The correct answer is (b). See explanation for the answer to question 2.

4. The correct answer is (b). Timeshare was an innovative and exciting idea that was poorly implemented. Initially, there were few government controls over timeshare sales, which allowed for numerous misrepresentations and high-pressure tactics. Additionally, the various exchange programs didn't work well and there was little demand for resales. However, timeshare is an investment in real estate. It is a form of condominium that comes with a deed for the number of weeks purchased and condominium documents. Therefore, answers (a), (c), and (d) are incorrect.

5. The correct answer is (c). This is a tough question and has been the subject of much controversy. The outer wall of the condominium is a common element governed by the rules and regulations of the association. However, the signals to satellite dishes are governed by federal law and it has been argued in court that condominium documents, which are a creature of state laws, cannot override federal laws. As a result, the argument went, associations do not have the right to interfere with an owner's use of satellite dishes. As a result of these cases, there is now a specific federal law that, in part, states that condominium associations can regulate the placement of satellite dishes if the dish is placed on the common elements of the building. It is never a good idea to curse at the building manager, especially when you are in the wrong, therefore answer (a) is incorrect. The essence of community and, specifically, condominium living is that you sacrifice certain freedoms for other overall benefits.

6. The correct answer is (c)—common elements.

7. The correct answer is (b). This is a tough question. Since we know that a cooperative is not a real estate purchase per se, answers (a),

(c), and (d) cannot be correct. Therefore, (b) must be the correct answer. Although not an investment in real estate, a cooperative is still governed by a board of directors of which the shareholders of the cooperative are members. This structure is still lo- "

.... association are shareholders in a corporate entity and not, strictly speaking, owners of their individual units. The basis for its overall operations are found in private corporate law rather than in general real estate law, which incorporates many of the discriminatory safeguards. Thus, there is wider latitude for the boards to issue restrictive policies in the overall operations of the corporate entity.

10. The correct answer is (c). Maintaining the overall appearance of the building's common elements is the direct responsibility of the board of directors through the property manager. Complaining to either through the appropriate channels is proper. Every purchase of real estate should be regarded as an investment, regardless of whether the purchase was made as a personal residence or to lease or resell. The overall appearance of the building directly affects the value of your individual unit, and you should always be concerned about the value of your investment, even if you have no immediate plans to sell or refinance.

11. The correct answer is (b). A townhouse is more like a private home than a large apartment complex. A cooperative may serve the purpose, but the question indicates that you want to make an investment in real estate. A cooperative is technically not a real estate investment. A hotel-condominum is generally not purchased for residential purposes.

12. The correct answer is (a). A townhouse is most closely related to private home ownership because it is a single-family dwelling that is not part of a multifamily complex. However, neither is it a private home, because common walls attach the dwellings. However,

many townhomes offer private yards or decks and amenities such as tennis courts or swimming pools.

13. The correct answer is (d). A cooperative tends to be less expensive than a condominium because it doesn't tend to appreciate as well as a condominium. Also, you technically don't own your unit but, rather, are a shareholder in the building with an assigned right to occupy your apartment. This makes it less valuable than owning your unit outright.

14. The correct answer is (a). Timeshare works well where the owner has restricted times to take a vacation. If the exchange program works well, the owner can exchange his or her time for time in another facility worldwide, depending on availability.

15. The correct answer is (a). Townhouses are subject to community association boards of directors, but they tend to interfere less than association boards due to the fact that townhomes tend to lean toward the private-property sector as opposed to multicomplex dwellings, which must be managed more strictly.

16. The correct answer is (d). The big advantage of community living is the fact that you can get all the amenities you couldn't afford with a private house that does not belong to a community association. Some community associations have private houses as well as townhouses and condominiums, but the main feature is the fact that they contain common-element amenities.

17. The correct answer is (d). While some condominiums provide community barbeques, most have rules and regulations concerning large animals. Also, the rules may restrict the amount of people you can have, or the barbeque may simply be reserved by another unit owner. In addition, most fire codes prevent the use of barbeques on private terraces. Your best bet would therefore be a townhouse with a private yard, where you can barbeque whenever you please and invite your family and friends. There are generally no restrictions on pets.

18. The correct answer is (c). The key elements of a hotel-condominum are limited use by the owner and income production through the hotel program.

19. The correct answer is (d). Community living means respecting rules and regulations and the rights of others to enjoy their prop-

erty (and vice versa), both individually and within the common elements. It means living together and compromising individual freedoms for overall higher standards of living—including, more often than not, better and more varied amenities. If

·······, ··· they don't have mutters). Generally speaking, noise is not beautiful in community associations. You should consider a private home that is not subject to a PUD and community association.

20. The correct answer is (d). Location is an important factor but not the only factor. Answers (a), (b), and (c) are all factors you should consider.

21. The correct answer is (d). This is a tricky question, because proximity to your work may be an important factor to you personally, but it is not a generically important factor in real estate consideration as a whole. You may work in a commercial factory district, but that does not mean that living next door will make the property valuable to someone who works in the downtown banking area of the city.

22. The correct answer is (d). Perceptions of where the real estate investment is located provide insight as to how others view your investment. Other people's perceptions can act as a check on your own evaluation of a property.

23. The correct answer is (d). "Type of people questions" lead to such issues as race, creed, color, and national origin, and have no place in your inquiry. Most state laws prohibit brokers from answering questions related to race, creed, color, or national origin.

24. The correct answer is (d). Economic factors include all of the considerations listed and are relevant to your investigation of the investment.

25. The correct answer is (c). Location is an important consideration, but is not the only consideration. There is no single factor that

determines whether a real estate investment is optimum. Therefore, even a seemingly ideal location won't assure the best investment.

26. The correct answer is (d). You have several problems here. First,
the project is not completed so you need to assure yourself that the
developers are reputable and have sufficient economic commitment and wherewithal to complete the project. An uncompleted
project can cause delays in the appreciation of a real estate investment. Information such as which bank is financing the project,
other developments completed by this developer, and so on can
act as predictors of the developer's solvency and ability to complete
the project. In addition, the project is located in a remote area.
This may be very nice and rustic, but will it take longer to appreciate in value? Are there any other similar projects in comparable
remote areas that have been successful? Is this a well-known tourist
spot in general? You may assume that people buying here will not
be purchasing a primary residence. This is a more risky investment
at best, and you should investigate it carefully before making a
purchase.

27. The correct answer is (d). D illustrates investigation of the area,
perceptions, and economics of the purchase. Many cities throughout the United States have had successful redevelopment of former
warehouse and factory districts into residential areas comprising
condominiums and cooperatives, but just as many do not. As in
question #26, simply being told by a broker that the area is scheduled for redevelopment means virtually nothing. The local planning commission will be able to tell you if any developers have
applied for zoning changes or construction permits to build or ren-
ovate properties. That will provide information as to area redevelopment plans. Perceptions are also important here. Even if the area
is scheduled for redevelopment, what do residents think about it?
Is there general excitement about the prospect, do people think it's
a crazy idea? Once you have some sufficient information, you can
weigh the risks and make your decision.

28. The correct answer is (d). This is a hard question, because there
are elements of truth in each answer. Children are of paramount
concern, and parents often do things for the sake of their children
that they wouldn't normally do. Proximity to good schools is one

indicator to be considered in making a real estate investment, but it may be a short-sighted view. Children grow up, and as they go from primary to middle or high school, school proximity may become less of a factor, depending ~~ ~~ ^1 ~ ~

... . are still building new projects and spending big marketing dollars to make the sales. However, the area may be good enough to absorb the demand. Demographic figures available from the local government should tell you how many people are coming into the area and why. Are there jobs being created in this area? What is driving this spurt in growth? The investment may be good, but you need more information before making the decision. Choice (c) is not as silly as it may initially sound. If your spouse is the chief wage earner, it may be more important for your spouse to live closer to work. That is a personal consideration. Thus, (d) is the best answer. If the investment meets your needs, you should consider making the purchase. However, factor in the amount of construction going on in the area in general, and consider if there is anything distinctive about your community or investment that makes it stand apart from the others, such that if you have to sell or leverage it (obtain new or further financing) yours will be more marketable. Is the community where the investment is located a gated community? In other words, does it have security at the entrance, or can anyone drive through the neighborhood? Does the community have any other amenities such as tennis courts, swimming pool, or a community center, and how close to them is your townhouse? What are the common charges? Are they lower than other communities in the area? Does your townhouse have any special features, such as a double rather than single garage? Is it a corner property with only one attached neighbor? These are factors that, in spite of the amount of construction, would make your investment more competitive in the marketplace.

29. The correct answer is (a). Find out why the banks won't lend on this property. If the banks won't tell you directly, persist in your investigation. Ask other real estate brokers or mortgage brokers. Ask people who live or work in the hotel-condominium. Eventually, you will get the answer. Generally speaking, if banks won't lend on the property, it sends out the wrong signals about the investment, even if mortgage money is available from secondary sources. Answer (b) is wrong because it shuts the door on what may be an otherwise good investment without obtaining sufficient facts. Answer (c) may be your ultimate decision, depending on answer (a). The short-term results may be good, but ultimately, real estate should appreciate in value and this may not, depending on why the local banks won't touch the investment. Answer (d) is nonsense.

30. The correct answer is (d). You should consider buying the condo because real estate is always an investment regardless of the fact that you may be planning to use it for personal use. If the area is flooded with townhouses, the law of supply and demand will dictate that appreciation will be lower. If you are economically comfortable, and assuming the overall appreciation is greater than the increased mortgage costs, you should go for the condo.

31. The correct answer is (d). Look at the area, the perceptions, and economics of the investment.

32. The correct answer is (b). There is no guarantee that a purchase from a developer will increase in value, or even that the project will even be completed. That is why it is crucial that you do a through job of research prior to making a purchase. This will minimize risk and maximize the chances that the purchase will be a financial success.

33. The correct answer is (d). All of the items listed are things that a prudent and astute purchaser should do.

34. The correct answer is (c). There are no guarantees that a purchase from a developer will always be the best real estate investment. However, one of the benefits of buying from the developer is that you are getting a new unit with new appliances.

35. The correct answer is (c). The developer may have all the information you need, but there is no guarantee that he or she will disclose

it, especially if it is not in his or her interest to do so. For example, do you think the sales agent will tell you the bottom-line price he or she is willing to accept? Therefore, answer (a) is incorrect. Whether or not developers like real estate brokers personally, they

....w... (c) as indicated above is correct. A good broker can help you negotiate the best deal and will possess information that will help you make the most appropriate decision.

36. The correct answer is (d). When you purchase from a developer, you are trading the security of seeing a finished product for the best possible price. Research is the key to risk minimization.

37. The correct answer is (c). You should never ask questions based on race, creed, color, national origin, sexual preference, or age. However, certain states have laws relating to senior citizens projects where one owner of the property must be at least 55 years of age or more (depending on state law) to purchase. This is an exception, and in such cases, it is proper to ask about age restrictions.

38. The correct answer is (d). When you are told that a certain percentage of inventory is sold, you are within your rights to make further inquiries to ascertain exactly what that advertised percentage represents. It doesn't always mean what it says.

39. The correct answer is (c). Sales brochures are a marketing tool to convince you, the purchaser, to make the purchase. Whatever information they contain, within the limits of state law, are designed to present the project in its most attractive light. A sales brochure is no substitute for thoroughly researching a project.

40. The correct answer is (b). You can always make an offer. If you don't, the answer will always be no. Your offer, though, should be based on something other than gut instinct or some fantasy price you desire. This is often where a good broker can be of service. The broker might know the developer's bottom line and help you

present an offer the developer will accept. Answer (d) is tempting but incorrect. Sometimes, an offer will be below that which a sales agent can accept because of the constraints of the developer's own financing, but the banks generally do not control the developer when it comes to accepting an offer if the offer is reasonable.

41. The correct answer is (c). Uncle Herb and Aunt Ida may be lovely people but if they haven't bought a piece of property in 30 years, they probably don't have any useful information to contribute. Unless a family member has some direct expertise (your brother is a real estate broker in the same town or city where you are planning to make your purchase), it is best not to discuss you purchases with immediate family.

42. The correct answer is (b). In most cases, when you buy from a developer, it is in the preconstruction stage and you don't see the finished product. The advantage is, you get the pre-appreciation price. One advantage of buying a resale is that you see the finished product, both in terms of the unit itself as well as how the property functions and what the costs really are, as opposed to being estimated or projected. Answers (c) and (d) are wrong as well. Prices are determined by market value and appreciation of the property. A resale may indeed be more expensive than a new property, depending on various market factors. When purchasing a resale, the buyer generally has more ability to negotiate both price and terms than when purchasing from a developer.

43. The correct answer is (d). You don't have enough information. You also need to know the asking price of the apartment you want to purchase, how long ago other sales took place, whether the current market is a buyers' or sellers' market, and what the properties were listed for and how long they have been on the market.

44. The correct answer is (c). You have been told that it is a sellers' market and property has sold within six months' time, albeit for lower prices. However, there are only two properties left, and they are listed high. This indicates that the market is strong and there is not much supply. You can factor in the sales comparisons, or *comps*, somewhat, but at this point, you probably cannot rely on the comps to make a deal.

45. The correct answer is (b). In this case, you are told that the market is a buyers' market, indicating that the market is getting weaker—

there will more supply on the market. In this situation the seller's high price might not be realistic, and an offer based on the best comp should be accepted.

46. The correct answer is (d).

...answer is (c). A transaction broker represents the seller and the buyer and has a fiduciary responsibility to both parties to act honestly and with integrity by not disclosing information to either side that will jeopardize the other's position.

50. The correct answer is (d). If you are going to live in a property, the purchase should not only represent a good investment, but should be something both parties like and are excited about.

51. The correct answer is (c). The basic blueprint for your real estate transaction is found in the contract, which contains the rights and obligations of both the buyer and the seller.

52. The correct answer is (d). The basic elements of a contract are the offer, the acceptance, and valid consideration. Also, a contract must have a definite term of expiration.

53. The correct answer is (b). A contract that places obligations on both the buyer and seller is a bilateral contract.

54. The correct answer is (b). The purchaser of a resale unit has more bargaining power with regard to the contract because he or she is considered to be at an "arm's length" with the seller. Developer's contracts are more adhesionary and purchasers have much less bargaining power when purchasing from a developer.

55. The correct answer is (a). Although your attorney, broker, or association members may or may not be able to give you the answers you need with regard to amenities of the building, these are *always* found in the condominium documents.

56. The correct answer is (d). A limited common element is an area that you do not own but have exclusive control of. Thus, the

storage bin in the question is a limited common element because it belongs to the common elements of the building but it is exclusively assigned to the owner of the unit.

57. The correct answer is (b). The association has the power to promulgate rules and regulations in order to operate the building. Operating hours of amenities are lawful regulations unless they are unduly restrictive and have no rational explanation. Therefore, closing the pool at 7:00 P.M. may be inconvenient, especially to those who work late and want to take a swim in the evening, but it is not per se an unlawful rule.

58. The correct answer is (d). The HUD statement is like an itemized bill, but it cannot convey title. That is done only by a deed.

59. The correct answer is (d). Title insurance is an important part of your real estate acquisition. The title insurance company insures that you have good title to your real property or it will defend any claims against you in that regard, and compensate you if it loses the case.

60. The correct answer is (c). "Time is of the essence" puts the parties to a contract on notice that delays will not be tolerated and could place the delaying party in default of the contract.

61. The correct answer is (a). Your local banker is a safe and familiar place and may provide you with the best deal. However, that should only be your starting point. It may not be the best deal available. Grandma is tempting and may be the best deal but clinically, that can't be a correct answer.

62. The correct answer is (b). Mortgage brokers are not considered lending institutions. They merely find you the best deal for a commission.

63. The correct answer is (c). The underwriter generally has the final say in approving your loan. When a loan is approved by the bank, it is subject to verification and acceptance by the underwriter. You should always check the fine print to determine if the loan commitment is final or subject to an underwriter's approval.

64. The correct answer is (c). The overall package, not merely the interest rate, will determine if the loan is financially right for you. Such factors as length of time, monthly payments, and prepayment penalties should always be considered.

65. The correct answer is (d). The lending institutions will factor in not only your creditworthiness, but also the type and value of the property you are buying. They are going to be your partner, and lending institutions are risk averse. There are also premiums for larger (i....l..) l......   . .f.....

68. The correct answer is (b). Paying in advance to lower the interest rate is known as a buydown.

69. The correct answer is (d). You should be fully prepared at the closing.

70. This is a tricky one. The correct answer is (a). First, we are asking for the percentage profit, not the cash amount of profit, so (b) is not the correct answer, although it is the correct dollar amount of profit. Twenty-one percent is the percentage of profit if it were a cash deal (i.e., if the $75,000 profit were made on a cash outlay of $350,000 by the buyer), but the question indicates 80 percent financing, which means you only put down 20 percent cash, or $70,000. $75,000 profit on an investment of $70,000 is approximately 107 percent.

71. The correct answer is (d), all of the above. Moving into a condominium requires coordination and adherence to the move-in rules of the building. To attempt to circumvent these rules could lead to increased costs, expense, and aggravation, not to mention delays in moving in.

72. The correct answer is (b). The condominium documents state the flooring requirements. Failure to adhere to the rules could cause the management to order your work stopped until you comply. There have also been instances when the association ordered the entire floor removed and relayed in accordance with sound-proofing requirements.

73. The correct answer is (c). Your name does not need to appear on the permit (except as the owner of the unit). The contractor should

go to the city and obtain whatever permits he needs to perform the project. This ensures that he shares in the liability for the work and is permitted and insured.

74. The correct answer is (d). Plumbing, like electricity, will generally require the contractor to apply and receive a permit.

75. The correct answer is (b). You have to read the answers carefully. Answer (a) is not correct because the building's insurance will not cover your personal property located within the four walls of your unit. The building's insurance policy will only cover damages to the common elements of the building, such as the hallways. Answer (c) is not correct because the neighbor is liable to everyone. The neighbor's negligence was the proximate cause of the damages to both your property and the common elements. Answer (d) is not correct because your insurance will not cover damages to the hallway, which is a common element.

76. The correct answer is (b). Answer (a) is incorrect because the building manager works for the association and is concerned with common element problems. Your personal air conditioning unit is your personal problem. Answer (c) is incorrect because your homeowners policy does not cover air conditioning repairs. The homeowners policy might be involved if the unit was destroyed or vandalized, but repairs do not fall within its parameters. Answer (d) is obviously incorrect. Sweating it out in 100-degree weather could lead to serious health concerns, especially as the temperature in your condo could climb well above that.

77. The correct answer is (d). An association board has the right to demand that dishes be taken down from common element or limited common-element portions of the building in accordance with federal law. Answer (c) is incorrect because an association board cannot force you to purchase cable television—or to even own a television, for that matter.

78. The correct answer is (c), although the police might not agree, and this is a highly contestable issue. We are of the opinion that as a matter of law, anything that is unreasonable is, by definition, excessive. One persons delicacy is another's poison. Drums may be music to a drummer, but long, unending drum solos are reasonably not thought of as soothing. I would argue that beating drums all day long and having jam sessions all night long is creating excessive

noise. Condominiums are to be used for residential purposes, and what you have in this case is the use of the apartment as a recording studio. Consequently, that is outside the permitted use of the apartment. A restraining order prohibiting this activity could be right-

... (b). These people are well meaning but aggravating. It doesn't pay to argue with them, especially if they are right. I recall living in a condominium that had a rule that stated you must use one hand to pull the front door open while inserting your key in the lock. Most people (including me) simply put the key into the door and pulled it open from the key. I got caught doing this and endured a five minute lecture on why this could ruin the lock and how constantly replacing the lock cost everyone money. Point taken. I never pulled from the key again. Other rules can have more serious consequences. For example, glass bottles at pools are generally forbidden for fear of breakage and injuring people in an area where bare feet are the norm. Being called to task on this is legitimate and may merit a five-minute lecture or a fine.

81. The correct answer is (d). The mortgage is usually handled by the closing agent who represents the interests of the bank. Bankers and mortgage brokers rarely show up at a closing.

82. The correct answer is (b). You should upgrade your unit but only enough to make it competitive with other similar units on the market. You should neither overimprove it nor leave it in its old unkempt condition. Remember the model apartment. Make it appealing. You must assume that the buyer has no imagination and will not see its true potential.

83. The correct answer is (a). Your local broker can be a font of information, but it is up to you to make the final decision after you study the information.

84. The correct answer is (c). Flipping real estate involves selling the property prior to closing.

85. The correct answer is (c). The type of agreement you sign with a broker should be based mainly on whether there is cooperation or competition between the brokers. If there is cooperation, then an exclusive listing is called for. If there is competition, you want to have competing brokers for your sale, so you don't want to sign an exclusive right to sell. Usually, in areas governed by a multiple listing system, the area brokers cooperate with each other.

86. The correct answer is (d). Capital gains taxes on the sale of real estate can be assessed on U.S. citizens and foreign *investors*, but not on U.S. citizens or resident aliens who occupy their homes for two consecutive years as their principal residence.

87. The correct answer is (d). See answer 86.

88. The correct answer is (d). Terms and conditions belong in the contract.

89. The correct answer is (d). Choice (c) is definitely the wrong answer. The closing table is the last place you want to bring up unresolved issues. There should be no unresolved issues at the closing table.

90. The correct answer is (a). The buyer should have two sets of keys, the warranty deed, bill of sale for personal property, and title insurance policy.

acceptance, in contracts, 107
adhesion, contracts of, 117–118
adjustable rate mortgages (A.R.M.), 139
advertising
    for new property, 66, 68, 69–70, 71, 74
    newspaper real estate supplements, 83, 192
    in selling process, 190, 192–193
air conditioning
    appliance insurance and, 162
    in comparing properties, 47–48
    in resale properties, 81
air-quality samples, 48
alienation of property rights, 16
amenities, 6
    children and, 166
    in comparing properties, 43
    for condominiums, 8–9
    for developer properties, 59, 66
    for hotel-condominiums, 15, 16, 124
    policies regarding, 50
    for resale properties, 84–85
    in selling process, 180
    townhouse, 21
American Dream, home ownership in, 6, 79
amortization, negative, 139
announced special assessments, 53–54
antidiscrimination law, 10, 11, 100
appliances
    in comparing properties, 43, 45–46
    in developer properties, 65, 153
    insurance for, 161–162
    in selling process, 153, 187–188

application forms, 99, 100
appraisals, 3, 27, 133, 184–185
appreciation
    benefits of financing and, 148–149
    of community-style properties, 31
    of condominiums versus cooperatives, 10, 11, 12
    of developer properties, 58, 78
    of hotel-condominiums, 12, 14
    in hot real estate markets, 169–174
    price history and, 54
    of real estate versus personal property, 3
    of resale properties, 88, 89
    time needed for, 171–172
    of timeshares, 20
approval process
    cooperative, 10, 12
    policies concerning, 54
area, perception, and economics (A.P.E.), 33–40, 174, 175
    area, see area/location
    economics, 37–40, 134–137
    for new properties, 73–74
    perception, 33–37, 40
    for resale properties, 81, 89
area/location
    checklist for analyzing, 32
    in comparing properties, 42–43, 45
    example of, 39–40
    in finding properties, 29, 31–33, 40
    for new properties, 72
    overall, 40

Look for These Exciting Real Estate Titles at
www.amacombooks.org/realestate

A Survival Guide for Buying a Home by Sid Davis $17.95

A Survival Guide for Selling a Home by Sid Davis $15.00

Are You Dumb Enough to Be Rich? by G. William Barnett II $18.95

Everything You Need to Know Before Buying a Co-op, Condo, or Townhouse by Ken Roth $18.95

Make Millions Selling Real Estate by Jim Remley $18.95

Mortgages 101 by David Reed $16.95

Real Estate Investing Made Simple by M. Anthony Carr $17.95

The Complete Guide to Investing in Foreclosures by Steve Berges $17.95

The Consultative Real Estate Agent by Kelle Sparta $17.95

The Home Buyer's Question and Answer Book by Bridget McCrea $16.95

The Landlord's Financial Tool Kit by Michael C. Thomsett $18.95

The Property Management Tool Kit by Mike Beirne $19.95

The Real Estate Agent's Business Planner by Bridget McCrea $19.95

The Real Estate Agent's Field Guide by Bridget McCrea $19.95

The Real Estate Investor's Pocket Calculator by Michael C. Thomsett $17.95

The Successful Landlord by Ken Roth $19.95

Who Says You Can't Buy a Home! by David Reed $17.95

Your Successful Real Estate Career, Fourth Edition, by Kenneth W. Edwards $18.95

Available at your local bookstore, online, or call 800-250-5308

Savings start at 40% on Bulk Orders of 5 copies or more!
Save up to 55%!
For details, contact AMACOM Special Sales
Phone: 212-903-8316. E-mail: SpecialSls@amanet.org